A SCHOOL WHERE I BELONG

A SCHOOL
WHERE
I BELONG

CREATING TRANSFORMED AND INCLUSIVE
SOUTH AFRICAN SCHOOLS

Dylan Wray
Roy Hellenberg
Jonathan Jansen

BOOK**STORM**

ISBN: 978-1-928257-51-6
e-ISBN: 978-1-928257-52-3

First edition, first impression 2018

Published by Bookstorm (Pty) Ltd
PO Box 4532
Northcliff 2115
Johannesburg
South Africa
www.bookstorm.co.za

Edited by Wesley Thompson
Proofread by Sean Fraser
Cover design by mr design
Book design and typesetting by René de Wet
Printed by ABC Press, Cape Town

Fostering Civil Discourse - A Guide for Classroom Conversations
reproduced with the permission of Facing History and Ourselves.

CONTENTS

INTRO
DUCTION

Nobody saw it coming – the beginnings of public protests on the grounds of former white schools in South Africa. It is true that South African schools have a long-established resistance culture dating back to the earliest days of slave education, when running away from school was one such response to colonial education. There were the protests over food in the mission schools serving the black elite. And in the late 1970s, there were the heralded uprisings that started in Soweto and fanned out across the country. Yet never before had such protests engulfed some of the well-established white English schools, from Pretoria High School for Girls in the north to Sans Souci Girls' High School in Newlands in the south.

The protests came as a shock to the teachers and administrators at these schools. After all, it was elite English schools, the private, church-affiliated schools and the public schools that had first opened their doors to black learners. In that sense these schools were liberal, even progressive in some cases, and certainly different from the neighbouring white Afrikaans schools, where black student numbers remained very small and limited to those with a facility in the Afrikaans language.

As more than one commentator had observed, this was a South African paradox – as more and more black learners came into former white schools and indeed universities, the more was the pressure on such places of learning to transform beyond simply giving access to those long denied entry. Once a critical mass of black learners had been reached, there were both the numbers and the confidence to air grievances within the school (or university) environment.

For those who study the history and politics of education in South Africa, the emergence of protest cultures within former white institutions was nothing unexpected. Access was never going to be enough in a country with some of the most expensive schools in the world existing alongside mud schools. The long shadow of history hangs heavily over our educational institutions.

What sparked the protests was not unequal access or infrastructure but a different kind of injustice, the problem of school cultures. That is, having gained a physical place in former white schools, black learners were now pressing for social and cultural inclusion as well. And it started with something as simple and complex as girls' hair.

As a black parent, I have to say that I saw this coming a long time ago. My children were born in another country and by the time they reached school-going age they could attend the schools where we lived, which were former white schools. Both my son and daughter would cringe when I showed up at parents' meetings because I would ask the following questions: Why must my daughter learn knitting? My son in the school next door does not have to do this? Why is there no soccer at the school, only rugby, cricket and even water polo? Where are the black teachers? I would like my child to also see competent black educators as role models in the school. Why are the Monday-morning assemblies run like Christian services? Surely a public school should recognise in its practices the Muslim, Jewish and Hindu learners, as well as those who do not believe?

The responses were sometimes funny and sometimes infuriating. From the schools' point of view, they were doing black families a favour by allowing access in the first place. For years the political environment had given white South Africans a sense of racial ownership of society and of their schools. Schools stuck in that mindset really did expect, and some still do, that black learners, by being allowed to attend these schools, should be grateful and fit into the established culture.

And so the responses to my questions in six different schools from Durban to Pretoria were standard. Girls in this school have been knitting for almost a hundred years; and the jerseys they knit go to the underprivileged. We cannot allow soccer because we don't have enough grounds to accommodate other sports. We cannot find qualified black teachers but you'd be happy to know Mrs Vilakazi teaches Zulu at our school. This has always been a Christian school and all parents are told that our ethos and values are based on Christian principles. The majority of our parents are Christian. And by the way, children have the choice of not attending assembly if it goes against their religious beliefs; they can stay in their classrooms.

But do not for one moment think that the defence of the cultural status quo at former white schools was made only by white parents and their governing bodies. At one of the Durban schools, where I asked for more black teachers, it was other black parents – Indians specifically – who responded angrily that they brought their children to this Westville school **because of** the white teachers there.

These six schools could neither understand that their cultures were exclusionary and that simply accommodating those from different social, cultural and political backgrounds was not enough; nor could they foresee, until it was too late, that sooner or later there would be a political price to pay for their closed-mindedness.

Nor did they understand that century-old practices no longer suited the white girls and boys in the late 20th or early 21st centuries. Demanding a certain skirt length from girls or short-cropped hair from boys were antiquated practices. The sometimes-authoritarian pedagogy inside classrooms was at odds with democratic precepts. Forms of discipline, or punishment, more accurately, belonged in another era. Forcing girls, other than the seniors, to sit on a cold cement floor during school assemblies not only carried risks for student health during chilly winters, but was also just old-fashioned nonsense that treated high school learners like children rather than adults-in-the-making.

But if white learners and their parents, often alumni of these schools, tolerated these practices, the new class of black learners would not. Now the schools had another problem: whereas white learners would experience the regulations on hair dress as simply antiquated, black learners would experience the same rules as racially offensive. And in a country with three centuries of racial discrimination built into the social fabric, any defence of these compound practices was going to be inadequate if not also provocative. Which brings us to the question: How should schools respond?

The first and more common response is to lay low, to pretend nothing happened, and to maintain these exclusionary practices. In other words, respond only if and when required but hope for the best – that these are other schools' problems. Black and white parents prefer white teachers. All parents enjoy the high standards set by the school. The school's academic track record is what really counts. If they don't like it here they can go elsewhere.

This is of course playing with fire and reflects poorly on school leadership in a changing country. One thing is certain: these protests will continue and become more common across former white schools and universities. As we have seen since the hair protests, black learners at elite schools have started to call out teachers for snide racial remarks. Often these everyday racist comments about Indians or Africans are dressed up as humour; boys will laugh it off at elite private schools: "Oh you know Mr X, that's how he is." Learners not being allowed to speak their mother-tongue African languages on the school grounds, a long-standing practice, has become an explosive issue at some schools. Black parents themselves are hyper-vigilant, and will use social media to expose the cultural or instructional segregation of their children. Clearly schools have to adopt new practices that foster greater inclusion in the school environment.

Does this mean that anything goes? That letting up on school discipline or regulations means that school culture will implode? I don't think so. At another Pretoria high school, on the poorer west side, the learners demanded to swear skinny jeans and not the restrictive school uniform; in that case there was a helpful self-correction – the media and the public took a harsh view of such opportunism. Most South African parents are concerned about order, discipline, and a predictable timetable, so those traditions at former Model-C and private schools that uphold these are important. But that does not mean that once physical access is gained, social and cultural recognition do not matter.

A different kind of response has been to take on the challenges of change presented in these recent crises. Here, school governors and principals have approached universities, non-governmental organisations and education change agents to help them make sense of and respond proactively to such crises. These leaders recognise that it is better to deal with problems of racism and exclusion during peace times than when the crisis hits. They invite learners to reflect on existing practices and to propose changes to what is taken for granted in the everyday life of schools. They are confident within their own skins and invite scrutiny and review from critical but supportive outsiders.

This book has been written for such school leaders who seek to deeply transform their schools even as they continue to set high standards for academic achievement. It is a book for teachers and school leaders who know that inclusion and achievement, recognition and results, equity and excellence, are not mutually exclusive ambitions in education. But these leaders also recognise that such transformation must be managed and informed by the best thinking available on how to change our schools.

I believe that this book, the first of its kind, will assist schools and school authorities to turn the crisis into an opportunity that benefits all our children.

Jonathan Jansen
Distinguished Professor of Education
Stellenbosch University
February 2018

WHAT

TO EXPECT FROM

THIS BOOK

Over the last few years we have been working with principals, teachers and parents across the country who are engaging with issues of transformation at their schools. Together we have explored a few critical questions:

- What are the implicit and unconscious biases school staff hold that are shaping our school cultures and impacting on the learning environments we seek to create in our country?
- Are the structures, codes of conduct and behaviours in our schools truly contributing to creating nurturing, inclusive environments where each young person feels seen and valued for who they are?
- Are we creating emotionally literate environments where our teachers have the skills to recognise their own biases and the feelings of marginalisation that some learners feel in schools?
- Are our schools, as they are presently, really preparing our learners to navigate a world that is increasingly diverse?

These are the questions that have guided us in this book.

In writing A School Where I Belong, we sat down with principals, teachers and former learners and captured their reflections and experiences on film. A selection of these interviews is included on the DVD that accompanies this book. All of the 89 videos will be available on the website www.aschoolwhereibelong.com along with a growing collection of resources, strategies and ongoing reflections and insights from the authors.

We need to note two things about the interviews.

Firstly, we have not included the full names of the interviewees, nor have we identified the schools they are connected to. We chose to do this so that what they share is not confined to one particular school or individual. We chose to share these interviews because they represent the sentiments, views and experiences of many people we have engaged with over the years.

Secondly, we chose to only interview former learners. We wanted to understand their experiences once they had left school and had time to reflect on their high school years. It also would not have been fair to interview learners currently in school.

We urge you to take the time to sit down, press play and listen to these experiences. Too often we do not make the time to truly listen and to hear what is being said. These people, we believe, are worth making the time for.

In writing the book, we chose to focus mainly on former Model-C and private schools because this is where much attention has been drawn. This doesn't mean that other schools do not have similar issues of exclusion and belonging. We believe that the lessons drawn from what is happening in one group of schools can be transferred to all schools. But it is also important to talk very specifically about former Model-C and private schools because, by and large, these are schools that have been successful. But if they do not transform, that success will be diluted and ultimately these schools will offer schooling that is no longer relevant or useful to young people of the 21st century.

There is no one-size-fits-all for school transformation. Each school has its unique history, culture and context, which influences how transformation can and does take place. But our review of international research and practice, as well as our own extensive experience in working with schools nationally and internationally, has led us to conclude that there are six things schools should be doing as they transform to become more diverse and inclusive. Schools should be *Facing the past*. They should be *Deliberately including*, and focusing on the need to be *Battling bias*, especially within the adults on campus. Schools need to be *Seeking difference*, management needs to be *Leading for change* and, in the classrooms, teachers need to be *Fostering civil discourse*. The first part of the book looks at these areas in more detail.

The second part of the book, *Where to begin*, provides practical steps to continue or strengthen the process of transforming a school to ensure that all learners feel that the school is a place where they belong.

This book requires not only reading for understanding, but also reading for reflection on personal beliefs and professional practice. It is intended primarily for educators and school leaders, such as members of the Senior Management Team and School Governing Body. But, we also hope that parents read this book. Parents shape the views of the young people schools are tasked to look after and develop. If parents are on board, a school's transformation journey is made that much easier. We hope that parents will find a deeper understanding of the key issues facing a school's transformation journey and that it may give substance to the feelings of alienation and exclusion they may have felt in their children's school environment.

This book is not meant to contain all the answers. In fact, sometimes it may raise more questions than you had before reading it. It is meant to start and further the conversation. It is meant to provide insights for reflection through the research we share. It is meant to provide an opportunity to hear the voices of the young people who pass through our schooling system, the educators who teach there and the principals who lead them. For us to hear their concerns, to see their struggles and to catch a glimpse of the hope they offer.

Dylan Wray and Roy Hellenberg
Cape Town
April 2018

WHO
IS FEATURED IN THE BOOK AND VIDEOS

Angelique

"I'm Angie. I graduated in 2013. I come from a co-ed school in a suburban area. It was a great experience, essentially. It was very fun being there. I enjoyed it. They exposed you to a lot of things that you wouldn't normally be exposed to, like our international tours and stuff like that. But ja, it was quite a nice school that I went to."

Dominique

"My name is Dominique. I went to a private school which is one of the best schools in the country. It's notorious for catering for the privileged in society. So in terms of the demographics at our school there was a very, very, very, very, very small proportion of people of colour at the school."

Markus

"My name is Markus. I am a PhD student based in London. I went to a private school, a church school. I matriculated in 2011."

Nabeel

"My name is Nabeel. I finished my degree at UCT (University of Cape Town) at the start of this year with my Honours. I matriculated in 2012 from an all-boys' school."

Olerato

"I am Olerato. I went to a co-ed, Catholic high school in Pretoria. It was very, very religious and also quite elitist in a way. It was a school mostly for black students, and, well, international students."

Sizwe

"My name is Sizwe. I matriculated in 2015. I currently study at the University of Cape Town. My school was an all-boys' school, very into sports. It was almost like a military kind of school. You have to be dressed in a certain way, your shoulders up straight when you're walking, when you're talking to someone. It was a very nice school, I'd say. It was a very diverse school as compared to the rest of the schools around the area."

TEACHERS

Leah

"My name is Leah and I've been teaching for five years. For four I was teaching at an international school and I'm currently teaching in a private girls' school. I'm 32."

Sue

"I am Sue and I have taught in state schools, my passion being History teaching. But since 2000 I have been at a private girls' school that provides an education for girls from the age of 3 to the age of 18. It is in a predominantly white suburb.

I am heading up the curriculum development at the school, so I am looking at the content of subjects and methodologies that are used."

PRINCIPALS

Meneer

"My name is Meneer. I am the headmaster of a traditional boys' school. The school was established in the 1930s and since then, up until 2013, it was only white headmasters. In fact, I'm the first black headmaster in the school. Many of the learners are blacks. I think there's only one white kid at the moment. In terms of the demographics I can say it's predominantly black."

Murray

"I am Murray. I am the principal of a public co-ed school. Our pupil body is virtually 100% black and coloured, typically middle- to lower-class backgrounds, living in townships or informal environments. The school is five years old."

Shaun

"I'm the head of a medium-sized boys' school. It's a school that's got a predominantly white population, although that is changing over time. At present we're in the region of 68% white kids to approximately 32% black and coloured kids. It's a school that is highly academic in its approach but also has a very broad and active sporting profile."

Shirley

"I'm Shirley. I'm the principal of a girls' school in the Cape Town area. It's a traditional old school and it's a government school, and I've been a principal for about 19 years. It is a multi-cultural school. It was, obviously, a traditional old white school, and over years it has transitioned into a school which has a fantastic South African spread."

Tony

"I'm Tony, and I'm the principal of a South African school. I have been a principal for just over 14 years now in two different schools. The first was a co-ed school, and I'm currently at a traditional boys' school. So that's me."

ABOUT THE AUTHORS

Dylan Wray

Dylan is co-founder and director of Shikaya – a non-profit that supports teachers and school leaders to ensure that young people who leave school are critical thinkers and compassionate, engaged, democratic citizens. Dylan has worked globally as a teacher, facilitator, materials developer and author, and is co-founder of FutureProof Schools.

Roy Hellenberg

Roy has served on the senior management teams of two top traditional boys' schools in South Africa. He has special interest and expertise in education in post-conflict societies, and has worked with Shikaya and Facing History and Ourselves over the past 11 years in equipping teachers to develop inclusive classrooms that encourage critical thinking and democratic practice. Roy is also a co-founder of FutureProof Schools.

Jonathan Jansen

Jonathan is Distinguished Professor of Education at Stellenbosch University. He served for many years as Vice Chancellor of the University of the Free State. He has a formidable reputation for transformation and for a deep commitment to reconciliation in communities living with the heritage of apartheid. He holds an impressive collection of degrees and awards, including the Education Africa Lifetime Achievement Award.

1

FACING
THE PAST

We need to face our past with honesty and courage. Until we face the fact that many of our schools weren't just silent bystanders but indeed active participants in the oppression of others, we cannot see a future in which we have a responsibility to educate for all and ensure that everyone in our schools feels at home.

"We can say, 'All right, we were a white school, come to us and fit in with what we believe in,' or we can say, 'We were a white school, and, while we cannot change the past, we recognise that that was an unjust system that we were part of, and in order for us to go together into a just society going forward we have to acknowledge that what was there was unjust.'"

Tony, **Principal**

WITH HONESTY AND COURAGE

The past does not lie quietly down to rest. Even when we hope we have tucked it in tightly, it murmurs, and as we are discovering, sometimes it stirs, wakes up and is not happy.

Through university students bringing down Rhodes and fees, and through girls tired with racially offensive policies at schools in Pretoria and Cape Town, South Africans are being forced to look back in order to simply understand today, let alone what will happen tomorrow. We are uncomfortably discovering that there is more of our past still to face, more of our history still to talk about, and more legacies still to acknowledge and respond to.

If we are to really hear the loud voices of these young people, we have to remember that our education system was built on a racially divided and unfair past. The legacy of apartheid and 300 years of colonialism reinforced a persistent message – that you could divide humanity into those who were allowed to achieve great things and those who were not. White South Africans were given better schools with better facilities and more opportunities to achieve those great things. University access was reserved for white South Africans, with higher-level thinking and deep theoretical reflection thought to be their exclusive domain.

Today, former white schools still have more resources and better facilities than poorer schools, and their success, based on a history of privilege, reinforces the message about who can achieve great things. Their well-maintained buildings and sports fields are still located in neighbourhoods that are wealthier. Most who enter and succeed in tertiary education come from these schools. As we have been reminded through the Fallist protests, access to universities remains out of reach for the majority of young South Africans.

There needs to be an understanding and acknowledgement of how these structures, formed to support a colonial and then an apartheid system, continue to exist, and how the perceptions created during this period of oppression continue to be ingrained in the cultures of many schools.

The Truth and Reconciliation Commission was a national project, but surely it was ultimately meant to become a community process where we, as South Africans, could look at all our institutions and begin to ask uncomfortable questions of ourselves? There were hopeful expectations that at some point we would turn to education and ask, "How did our schools perpetuate an unfair and discriminatory system and society? How did this school encourage it? What needs to happen next?"

Very few schools have willingly begun this difficult conversation. Few have looked back on that past and spoken about how they as an institution, or as part of a racially hierarchical education system, excluded other young South Africans from also achieving great things – and not just accepted that the law gave them no choices. Few have admitted how they might have accepted that only white South Africans could participate, and how sometimes, they chose not to be concerned that no one else was participating.

Hardly any schools have had the courage to say, "Whether we were present at the time or whether we are new to this school, this institution carries a legacy that we have to take responsibility for today." Fewer have asked, "How do we use the privilege given to us by the past to build a school that no longer excludes those who live too far or are too poor, where everyone will feel like they belong?"

We need to face our past with honesty and courage. Until we face the fact that many of our schools weren't just silent bystanders but indeed active participants in the oppression of others, we cannot see a future in which we have a responsibility to educate for all and ensure that everyone in our schools feels at home.

"I think it's important for all of us to acknowledge the past and I don't think we can escape that. The universities at present, in particular UCT, are going through a truth and reconciliation sort of process. You know, our school is part of a system that existed, an education system that existed in the past as well. We were part of a process that said, 'You can only take white boys' at one stage.

When our school was formed at the end of the 19th century, one of the conscious reasons for its formation was to find reconciliation between Afrikaans- and English-speaking families after the Anglo-Boer War, which was considered a real problem. There was this rift between Afrikaans-speaking people and English-speaking people, and there was a very conscious attempt at the time to bring the two communities together. I think when the possibility opened for white schools to start admitting pupils of colour, our school was a very early adopter. But I suppose what we need to do would be to really dig into the past.

It's certainly a language that's entered into the conversation around our vision and what's been written into that as well. We're very conscious of the fact that we're a school that has mostly catered for white privileged kids and that we have a responsibility to change that.

I suppose one could rewrite the history books to make a statement of that sort. I don't think anybody in our school system, certainly, would have any objection to owning up to the fact that we were a white elitist school at one stage. I think what's most important to me and to the school is to change where we are right now and to be different now."

Shaun, **Principal**

DUSTING IT OFF

It is hard to be an adult who grew up during the apartheid era in South Africa and not still carry some of its dust. This is South Africa, after all. We have many dirt roads and the winds of change keep returning strong, scattering dust everywhere.

Just as the past has shaped our education system and the ethos and culture of our schools, so too has history shaped the people who work in these buildings. Given that the average age of teachers in South Africa today is around 35 years, most teachers currently in schools were themselves learners in a racially divided and unequal system. Some were even teachers then. They all bring some of that history into their classrooms.

For more than 15 years we have been running the programme *Facing the Past – Transforming our Future* in partnership with Facing History and Ourselves in Boston, USA. Through many workshops, seminars and conferences, we have brought together hundreds of teachers from all backgrounds and ages to explore their identity, how they see each other and the impact this country's past has had on us, how we teach and, even, where we teach. These have been unique spaces of learning where black, white, foreign national, female, male, old and young teachers faced each other, shared their history and stories, listened and, for many, heard for the first time. Crucially, teachers were given curriculum support to change their classrooms into inclusive and safe spaces where vigorous debate could be encouraged.

When we were planning for the very first *Facing the Past* workshop in 2003, we were concerned about how teachers would cope sitting across from each other, black and white, exploring the painful history we have lived through. We knew that the process would open doors that had been purposefully shut many years before. We knew that teachers of different races and backgrounds sitting in the same room, exploring a past that affected them each so differently, could open wounds, lend weight to guilt, and echo indifference.

> **"Never underestimate the power of a room full of teachers to support themselves."**

We were concerned at our ability to create a space safe enough to honour and value those who would be in the room, so we went in search of help from trauma counsellors. But we didn't get very far. Our first meeting was with Paul Haupt, who at that time was working for the Institute for Justice and Reconciliation. We had come to get his advice, and were hoping he could be in the room and manage the trauma we feared to face. It wasn't to be. Not because he hadn't offered his help, but rather because of what he had told us. He said (something like), "You don't need to have trauma counsellors in the room with you. You have teachers. Teachers spend their days managing the emotions, feelings and reactions of classrooms filled with 20, 30, 50 young people". And then he added (verbatim), "Never underestimate the power of a room full of teachers to support themselves."

We gave up looking for trauma counsellors. We have never underestimated the supportive power of teachers. Although the past has been painful and the conversations raw, a trauma counsellor has not been needed. Of course, we have had to guide and facilitate a process and conversation. But when it came to hearing one another's stories and reflecting on their own identity and choices, the hundreds of teachers who we have worked with were able to speak, and they stayed in the room listening, uncomfortably and cathartically. Our work was to invite them to begin the conversation. These conversations are needed now more than ever.

Much of what we have witnessed through this opportunity is echoed in what these three teachers said about the process:

"I know how indoctrinated I was, so people who are older are much more so than me. That has to influence their teaching, irrespective of what race they are. And if we're not critically looking at how it is that who we are influences how we teach, then we're just perpetuating either hatred, maybe indifference towards the other, whoever they are, and then how do we possibly create a new way of being?"

"I think it was difficult preparing myself for that type of lesson … because I needed to search my own heart for my own prejudices and my own thoughts and be confronted with my own inadequacies … Just thinking through where I was at the time. How the laws that I wasn't even aware of at the time as a child impacted on me. [This] was actually harder than understanding what the law meant."

"The stories of the 'white' teachers especially were significant. I think there are many generalisations that this group had no need to complain and that they all benefitted from the old system. I think there is also a stereotype that those who did suffer must just get on with it, move on. What the *Facing the Past* workshops have done is to give us space and acknowledgement that our stories are powerful too. This of course is mirrored in what we then do in our classrooms."

When schools became multi-racial in 1991, very few planned for the hard work that would need to be done to recognise that teachers are people who carry their history, prejudices and ways of being into the classroom. Very few since then have proactively supported all their teachers to be more reflective of how our past has shaped them. Few, especially those with racially homogenous staffrooms, actively made the effort for staff to learn with and from teachers very different from themselves with very different stories to tell. Most of us simply moved on. Doors were opened, new curricula were adopted and teachers were trained to teach it. But teachers, on the whole, were not trained and supported to move from a racially divided system into one that sees everyone as equal. They were not supported to transform within a transforming education system.

On the third day of that first five-day *Facing the Past* seminar, we invited the teachers to have a silent conversation. They walked around the room, quietly reading short stories from South Africans living under apartheid that we had put up on the walls on big sheets of paper. The stories we chose represented the mix of experiences, colours and complications that is the history of South Africans living during apartheid. We asked the teachers to read the stories and then respond by writing down their feelings, reflections and thoughts on a large sheet of paper. These could be words, questions, even drawings. They could respond in any way and to anything in the story.

As they walked around the room, reading the stories and responding, they began to have a conversation with each other. A conversation in writing, between our history, our present, and – because these were all teachers – our future as well. It was one of pain, guilt, and healing. It was one that had been avoided often, never revisited, but needed all along.

In response to a story, a teacher wrote the following about her own history:

"My father was lighter skinned than the rest of us. People thought he was white. My father once took us to a 'Whites Only' beach. The whole family drove to the beach. We got there and the police were standing at the turn-off. They stopped the car. They said they would allow my father to go in but not 'the maid and her kids'. He turned the car around and drove home. All of us, including my father, cried all the way home."

In silence, a teacher who read this picked up her pen, drew the outline of a footprint next to what she had read and wrote:

"I left my footprints and realise I have always been allowed to leave them. Where I place my feet, my smelly, sweaty feet, has never been legislated against. I have never had to tread lightly."

Both teachers needed that moment. One to speak of shame, humiliation and hidden pain, and to be heard. The other, to recognise, to acknowledge and to let it be said that history had offered her privilege. Both needed to face some of the past, and they needed to do it together. While it was a conversation without a voice, the past was no longer silent.

They, like so many others over the years, have needed and valued these moments. Each returned and still returns to classrooms of young people who are waiting to be guided safely into an unknown future, each covered in a little of the dust that their teachers inadvertently brush off.

"These issues, these learnings, this reflection, is not something we do for the children; it's something the adults need more than anybody. We have to live it and that's hard sometimes as adults. You're a little bit more stuck in your ways and a little bit less flexible than young people. But slowly and gently it's very important to do similar work with the adults. Adults, we're slower to move. We might not see massive changes, but just to have a bit of openness, you know, to either sharing your own stories or learning a little bit about each other, is very important, I think, in the school."

Murray, **Principal**

TAKING ON TRADITIONS

Most schools with a few decades behind them have developed traditions that are a part of the life of the school and were intended to help shape the values and culture of the school. These traditions are found in events, commemorations, and in the names of school houses, buildings, and other spaces in the school.

Traditions at their best are intended to allow us to identify with, to approve of, and to become part of something bigger than us, something that we can leave as a legacy. Through participating in traditions, we understand that we are serving an institution and not ourselves, drawing us as human beings out of our self-obsession to an acknowledgement that community is more important. In participating, we contribute towards something that will outlive us. Every human being wants to leave a legacy. Participating in a tradition, upholding a tradition that builds community, is that kind of legacy. So, traditions can be very important. But they still need to be examined in light of how we have just defined their value.

For many schools, traditions emerged through an understanding of a world substantially different from today. In order to remain successful and relevant, schools need to transform, and to understand how to adapt to a changed society.

For schools that have been around for more than three decades, we need to look at customs rooted deeply in our colonial and sometimes racist past. We must look at the awards we give and the names we honour in giving them. We need to look at names of houses that reflect the heritage of the school – a heritage that likely holds negative connotations for some young people coming into the environment. We must look at how these traditions may silence some histories and champion others.

Traditions are only valid when they build the values of the entire community. Otherwise, they are just things that have been around for a long time. Everything that is old is not necessarily valuable.

This is not saying that schools that have been around for a while are not adapting and changing. There are many that are, in different ways. Some of these are highlighted in this book. Some have grasped (or are beginning to grasp) that the skill is understanding what needs to be preserved from the past and what needs to and can be moulded differently. They are looking inwards to understand that which is foundational and doesn't change no matter what happens in society and those things that are adaptable and can be morphed to satisfy the demands and the needs of a very different world.

... the skill is understanding what needs to be preserved from the past and what needs to and can be moulded differently.

School leaders need to relook at traditions. They need to guide a process that ensures the traditions their schools hold onto are those that include everyone. They need to be able to identify and value those traditions that make everyone feel like they belong and are a part of the school.

We need to introduce new traditions, new ways of being, and new values that are useful in the 21st century. Like those before us, we need to foster traditions that cement these values and build community among and from us. These traditions will bind future generations and give us a sense of stability in an unstable world.

"One of the issues that came up was that there was a feeling that some of the names we had in our school, the traditional, colonial names, were no longer appropriate. For me as well as many others, we couldn't understand that the colonial nature was that difficult for the learners. It was part of our history. But through all of these discussions, it emphasised the fact that when those names were there, many of my girls couldn't come to the white South African school that I ran. I think that was a huge step for me – that it no longer actually mattered what the name was as long as we all felt comfortable with [it]. And that really was a huge shift because I was very much against name changing to start with because I was very traditional.

You know, sometimes it's difficult to put your finger on what makes a person shift, but for me, I think it was just listening and listening and listening, and hearing more and more why people felt how they did. And so often, I think, in our world we hear that people want to do something but we don't stop to listen as to why they want to do it. So the more I heard why, and the hurt that people felt, the more I realised that I could be more in their shoes and look at it from a different angle. And so the shift for me became, 'So what is a name? Is it actually the essential part of the school?' And no, it isn't.

There are girls that have never had the chance to be part of some of the old traditional schools with the resources they've had, and I do think we need to acknowledge that. An interesting thing happened just this week. We were talking about Founders' Day and how we could acknowledge not only the founding of our school, which is the traditional model, but to in some way acknowledge that there were many people who couldn't attend our school, and there were many people who struggled, who went through the struggle, who were activists, to get to the point of allowing the girls who are currently there [to attend]."

Shirley, **Principal**

2

DELIBERATELY INCLUDING

Teachers can begin to undo some of what our history has left us. But only if they believe it matters and that they can do something about it. The same teacher who is able to explain the behaviour of a child when they discover that a parent is an alcoholic or the family is going through the crisis of a divorce, struggles to understand the legacies of generations. She struggles to see that the messages passed down of who is superior and who is inferior affects a learner when they walk into her classroom. She struggles to see that the past, like the child's family circumstance, matters.

"I think the anger that these past pupils express is that the school didn't recognise who they were and where they came from, and I think that's the challenge to us. This is why I say it would be patronising for us to try to help kids to fit in, because that's not what I think is being asked for. It's not about helping people to fit in; it's about helping the school to change, to become a place where everybody fits in, and so that's, I think, the real challenge."

Shaun, **Principal**

AWOKEN AND BETRAYED

The protests in schools that started over hair-dress policies in Pretoria in 2016 and soon spread across the country came as a rude awakening to many teachers and principals at former white schools. Angry, fed-up voices were shouting at them, "You have not recognised me! You have never seen me! You've turned me into a 'school X girl' and you've turned me into a 'school Y boy' and you've denied my difference, my culture, my background, everything about me. You have turned me into something that is not who I am."

These are difficult things to hear.

These young people were, and are, rising up because they felt completely cheated by an educational process in which they trusted their teachers to guide them along a road of self-discovery that would help them achieve a personal sense of fulfilment. They were told that their education would not only be about the content of the curriculum, but also about the books they would be asked to read and the cultural engagements and discussions they would have in class. This would help them realise a value system that would develop them into full, rounded people. And they believed it.

Then these young people woke up one day and discovered that the way they spoke, the way they wore their hair, the places they went to and the interests they shared, were not an expression of themselves but rather of what others expected of them, an expression of a very different culture. They were left with a deep sense of betrayal – that the teachers they loved and whom they hoped would guide them, had brought them to this unfamiliar place.

But on the other side, the teachers, many of whom were experienced and intuitive educators, who had helped thousands of young people mature into fully developed, responsible adults, also felt betrayed. They believed they had made the effort to step out of their comfort zones to ensure that learners from other cultures, religions and races would feel accepted and welcomed. They felt they had treated everyone equally. "I don't see colour," they may have said. They had guided all learners under their care on the right path – the same one that other learners had successfully followed for so long. But now their learners had turned around and said, "What you've done to me I don't appreciate. No thank you, Ma'am!"

One awoke and both betrayed.

But it is the teachers who are the adults in this relationship of trust and learning. The task now falls to us as adults, teachers and principals, to turn the betrayal we may feel into reflection and action. Perhaps, with more awareness, there might be two awoken and both found trusting.

"I have memories of driving from where I lived to school. I lived in one of the townships and I used to wake up early in the morning just to get a bus so that I could be at school on time. Whenever I was driving from or to school I'd sit by the window and I'd look at the transition from where I was to where I was going. I'd notice a distinct change because the school is in a neighbourhood that is very fancy and very white. It has a certain level of respect with its name. As you move towards the freeway you can see the distinct lines of difference. The township is all dull and it's a mess. It was all messed up.

At first I didn't feel welcome as a friend in that space. But as I started building my accolades, or my achievements, I started becoming recognised. I used that to put me in those important seats where I was sitting. At a stage I felt like I was welcomed by those people. I felt like I didn't belong but I had a place there, a place of influence or, you know, just that I was seen.

But I had to lose a lot of things in order to be seen. You lose a lot of things. Like sometimes you have to adapt to a different accent so that they can hear you well. Sometimes you have to act a different way to your fellow brothers. You need to carry yourself with a certain posture. Sometimes you end up being a foreigner in your own environment, in your own home, because your twang is different, because you wanted to get that seat at that office. So you do lose a lot, you lose your culture, your beliefs, and your life becomes a challenge. You challenge how people act at home and you compare yourself to your peers. You think, for example, 'What would John say when I'm doing this?' Yet you were brought up to believe in that culture and that environment. It does change you. It does change you as a person.

Model-C schools weren't made for black people. We're visitors. We're visitors in the space because we're not made proud of our belongings, of where we come from. We are brought into a system that's created there and that's been there for years, because the school was standing from 150 years ago and nothing has really changed. Okay, a few things have changed; the demographics have changed and we've brought in a few black teachers. But it ends there.

There's still that stereotypical image of the white heterosexual male in the school who plays sport. The school still fits everyone into that category. You have to be that picture, even if you're black, you're Indian or whatever, you need to fit that picture of this white heterosexual male who plays sports and who's maybe good in academics – just a bit, maybe 50% is good enough – but you need to have that rugby body and all that goes with it.

Feeling like a visitor at a Model-C school also extended to sports. Soccer wasn't taken seriously at the school. The school was number one in the country for basketball for many years. But the basketball courts were of an atrocious standard. We had paint falling off, graffiti on the walls and everything. But when it came to rugby … you'd see that it was rugby season. The fields would be green and the workers would be constantly working on those grounds and making sure that everything was fine. The stands would be painted for war cry, for people to sit. They'd bring out chairs for headmasters and other invited guests. You could see where the school's finances were going: rugby and cricket. You could see very clearly that no attention was paid towards soccer and basketball.

What's common between soccer and basketball? They're both considered 'black' sports in South Africa. Black sports weren't considered important at the school. So again, it made me like a foreigner in a space.

Black people were not meant to be in that space. But if you want to survive, sometimes you have to play the game and be part of things. Sometimes you don't mean to get involved, you don't mean to change just to suit the system, but it becomes a subliminal thing, like an unconscious thing, you end up doing just that."

Sizwe, **Former Learner**

WHO AM I?
WHO HAVE I BECOME?

The teenage years are awkward years. Every teacher in a classroom of grade 9s knows this all too well. Psychologists tell us that teenagers struggle with issues of self-image and self-esteem. But in South Africa, in schools that are more multi-cultural, for some, the teenage years are more complicated.

We can all remember grappling with the uncertainty of who we are, the journey of establishing our own identity, the opportunity to test the morality and values our families passed onto us. At some point we asked, "Do I want to accept this? Is this me? Is this what's going to define me as a person?"

Before adolescence, we generally accept the values and teachings of our family as truisms, but during the teenage years, we begin to question, to challenge, and to find what seems to fit with us. With that comes a terrific amount of angst and uncertainty.

All kinds of things are happening to the body. Oestrogen or testosterone creeps in. Changes are happening that cause fluctuations in mood or in levels of aggression. This is further complicated when teens are thrown into an environment with a thousand other teenagers who are going through the same struggles.

The way teenagers cope with all of this, and remarkably they generally do, is the way that all human beings cope. They seek a group. They wander through these years and through the corridors of schools forming groups to identify with, to belong to, and to feel safe within and seen by.

In South African schools, another dynamic confronts some teenagers more than others and leaves them having to work harder to feel seen.

This is a country with a history of gross human-rights violations, where different groups have been told different messages over time. One group has been told for many generations, "You are better than everyone else. You are more intelligent. You have control over your world. You can access power, opportunity and privilege because of who you are." Generally, like those family truisms, values and beliefs that are only questioned when we become teenagers, most white South Africans have internalised this and have not held it as something external to be viewed, discussed or even changed.

It is equally naïve to believe that things will change by themselves with time. We have to recognise that teenagers in our schools, already grappling with a difficult journey of self-discovery, are struggling to unravel the legacies of the past. We have to acknowledge the complexity of the isolation that a young person of colour in South Africa feels in a space where they are not allowed to just be and to find themselves, where they have to try and fit in if they want to belong.

We have to recognise that teenagers in our schools, already grappling with a difficult journey of self-discovery, are struggling to unravel the legacies of the past.

What does it mean for boys and girls, already dealing with issues of identity, to be told, for example, that their accent is not good enough, that their accent is somehow an indication of their character and intelligence? What does it take away from them when they are forced to consciously or unconsciously adopt the accent of the dominant class?

Often, but not always, the pressures and demands placed on them are implicit – the way they wear their hair, what they speak about, what they socialise around and what they do over weekends. These things are determined by the dominant class and culture at the school. To fit in, to participate in the conversations of the dominant group and to feel included, some learners have to become someone else in order to survive.

Teachers can begin to undo some of what our history has left us. But only if they believe it matters and that they can. The same teacher who is able to explain the behaviour of a child when they discover that a parent is an alcoholic or the family is going through the crisis of a divorce, struggles to understand the legacies of generations. She struggles to see that the messages passed down of who is superior and who is inferior affects a learner when they walk into her classroom. She struggles to see that the past, like the child's family circumstance, matters.

Teachers have the skills to recognise this problem and address it. They are trained in pedagogical theory, in understanding how children learn values, how they absorb issues relating to integrity, how their characters are formed and how their thinking is shaped.

This is the job that teachers have been prepared for. They just have to believe it matters and that they can do something about it.

"I don't think that I lost a part of me. I really believe that you're meant to be where you're meant to be at a particular time. Me being at that school, even though the experience wasn't the greatest, I know that for me to be the person that I am now I had to have gone through that experience. And I think it made me a lot more secure and comfortable with who I am because I was forced to question that every single day when I was at that school.

My overall experience in high school was hard to sum up. I think it changes depending on what I'm going through at a particular time. But I think that it was a transformative one in terms of what I was able to learn about myself, about socioeconomic dynamics in the country and how that plays out in a very small group of people.

When I think of the dominant culture of the school, the first thing that comes to my head is whiteness. Whiteness. We used to make this joke, a few of my friends, when the walls of the school were painted. Every two years or so, the walls were painted. We used to say that the minute a dark spot gets spotted on the white walls it needs to be repainted so that the whiteness can be restored. It's also a religious school, religious in terms of on paper. I'd say wealthy and white. Wealthy and white.

Not everybody fitted into that dominant culture of the school. Me and my very close group of friends, we were all on scholarships. Our parents weren't able to afford the fees. You noticed from every grade there would be a group of black and coloured people that would become very good friends because it's almost like a 'We need to stick together' situation. So I definitely don't think that everybody fits into this stereotypical girl that goes to this school. That's something that we who didn't fit in had to work through. Being together sort of helped that navigation process of 'Where's my space? Where's my place in this environment?'

Being of a different class and race, it definitely heightened my questioning of my belonging within the walls of the school. I think that a lot of that reflection happened once I'd left, because at the same time I felt the need to assimilate a lot of the time and to pretend I felt comfortable when, in hindsight, I definitely did not.

I think it would be hard to pinpoint a particular moment at school, but I think generally feeling like an outsider, or a minority. I was not comfortable inviting my friends over to my house because I live in a predominantly coloured area, and most of my friends at the time lived in Constantia or Bishopscourt and had tennis courts on their properties. I don't know, what would they think of me if they come to my house?

I navigated through high school, obviously trying to figure out who I am, a teenage girl asking, "What is my place in this world?" Being in that school environment definitely made me question that a lot more."

Dominique, **Former Learner**

BODY SUITS

"Identity," says education psychologist, John Amaechi, "is not just something you come to know about yourself." It is also "the mirror self – the idea that your identity is made up in part by how other people see you".[1]

For those young people who come in as outsiders to the dominant culture of a school, how they are seen by others matters. This impacts on how they see themselves and their ability to truly find themselves. If adolescence is largely about this, then frankly, some children are losing out.

John Amaechi grew up in Manchester in England. He travelled to the United States to study, and while at university, discovered basketball. He was eventually inducted, as the only Briton, into the NBA Hall of Fame. He also happens to be the first openly gay NBA player. So he knows a lot about identity, finding himself, and fitting in. As an education psychologist, he also understands a great deal about how identity plays out in schools.

Amaechi describes how, when young people enter an environment where they suddenly lack the safety and support they need for self-expression, where they cannot be themselves and are forced to fit in, they put on a "body suit", an identity they construct in order to keep up appearances of fitting into the dominant culture:

> A lot of people think we need a safe environment because it is just about this warm and fuzzy experience that young people are supposed to have in education. And it's not really about

---

1 "John Amaechi Discusses Identity", interview with Facing History and Ourselves. Available at: https://www.facinghistory.org/resource-library/video/john-amaechi-discusses-identity (accessed 5 April 2018)

that. We need a challenging but safe environment because there is a very narrow strata, a very narrow bandwidth, where young people can be challenged and high-achieve emotionally. And when you are in that sweet spot, amazing things can happen, and when you are outside of it, there's very little chance of high achievement.

And what this does, when people are in environments that don't feel safe, that don't feel supportive, they end up coming to school, dressing themselves almost in a body suit, in a "you suit" – that is a construction designed to help them to blend in and fit, to pass, whatever identity item that you are talking about. It allows them to pass through and at least be invisible if not outstanding. The problem is that [they have] to dress up in a way that makes them uncomfortable, and a lot of people do this – a lot of teachers and principals will do this too. They have to code switch. They have to come to school with a different set of behaviours. And everybody knows the relief that you feel when you come home at night and it's almost like you unzip that suit and you can breathe again. You can finally take that big breath and relax. But you also know that you have to be an amazingly high-functioning person to be able to manage your day with that kind of suffocating suit on, and kids don't have this capacity.

So they come to school wearing this suit that allows them to fit and pass, and you're asking them to do these really high-level thinking and cognitive tasks in learning. And they can't do it, because they have no authentic connection; they are disconnected from the world of the school by this suit that protects them, they hope, and they are also suffocated by it.

They're just not going to risk unzipping and being seen for the first time as a person

> *"... teachers have to create this emotional space where it is safe but challenging, where people can be themselves."*

in a space where they think there is any chance, any risk to themselves or their identity or their person. And so it is very true that in the early stages of interventions that [are] really ideal situations people have to create, teachers have to create this emotional space where it is safe but challenging, where people can be themselves, where people can take chances and fail, where people can tell stories about them and reveal things about themselves without risk of derision, without fear of being marginalised. Without safety there is nothing, there is no learning.[2]

2 "John Amaechi Discusses Identity", interview with Facing History and Ourselves.

"From grade 1 to 7 in the junior school, I won't say I was mercilessly bullied, but I was bullied to a degree because I was thin, kind of scrawny. I wasn't good at sports, I wasn't good at academics … So I didn't fit the mould, and I think a large part is because I'm brown. Most of my friends were brown and Muslim as well.

Once I got to high school I realised, in grade 9 and 10, I sort of internalised self-acceptance at a school like that and I threw caution to the wind. I 100% gave in to what it is to be a boy at that school. I changed the sport I played. I used to love soccer. I played rugby, started gyming and all these things. So I had to mould myself to fit into it to gain some sort of social credit and credibility.

At our school there were the three racial groups. There were the white people (the most) the coloured people (a sizeable portion), and black people (five). Straight up, five!

Soccer was what the coloured people played. Once I got to grade 10 I was like 'I can't play soccer with these people' because I had to fit in. It dawns upon you as a kid what it means to be accepted. You don't want to be lonely, you don't want to be eating your peanut butter sandwich by yourself. So you have to pick a side, and that's the side that I picked ... I had to exert noticeable effort to fit the mould.

So if there are 160 boys in a grade and 30 of them are coloured and 5 to 10 of them are black, that grade will exude a white narrative of what it is to be accepted, what it is to be cool for a 15-, 14-year-old, or however old you are. Because they come from white spaces. Their parents, I imagine, are mostly white. They live in white areas, they're doing white things, and it's just different. When the scales are balanced so against people of colour for their ways of life, for their customs, their standards of beauty, their sport tastes, all these things ... When you are a minority, to be accepted into the culture of the school you have to give up on yourself, you really do, and for learners who are unapologetically black, Muslim, coloured, an 'other' in the school – I mean I have respect for any learner who can just be themselves like that.

I think of the history of people of colour who have worked so hard throughout colonial and apartheid oppression to be able to send their kids to schools like that, who must now hear their kid come home with a twang. I was ridiculed in my family for coming home with a twang, and the only reason I did that was to be accepted for three years in a school. What does that mean in the grand scheme of things? And so those kids who go there give up on their history, give up on their historical sense of self, give up on so much because the school demands that of them, and subtly so as well. Not that the school is going to whip you and tell you to 'speak a certain way' or 'comb your hair a certain way' or 'buy some types of clothes'. But you're going to feel weird if you don't, you know what I mean? Like I did."

Nabeel, **Former Learner**

"In Afrikaans classes or whatever, teachers would say, 'You can't speak African languages in my class.' You know, it's quite disheartening, really, that there was this trampling down of assimilation, especially within a school of predominantly black students. In that sense there were those teachers that I felt could have done a bit more in terms of ensuring that the space is reflective of who the students are. I think if the teachers would have allowed students to speak their own languages, for instance, things may have been different.

It would have allowed for a bit more individuality within that space. It would have allowed for an appreciation of the self, a more intrinsic fundamental appreciation of who you are and where you come from. Otherwise there is essentially a perpetuation of that culture of 'Oh, you have to speak English in a certain way', where some students are not as eloquent as other students because they came from a place where they were speaking predominantly their own languages, or the schools that they went to didn't focus necessarily so much on the English language. You arrive there and the school is almost fostering this thing of 'You are only good if you speak very good English'. It kind of contributes to the fact that a lot of students rather ended up struggling with issues of self-confidence and also exclusion, because essentially not all of them could speak the way I'm speaking right now. That became a problem. There are micro things that add up that they could have addressed.

If they did allow students to zone into more parts of their own cultures, it would build more of a holistic individual who is able to account for and identify with the different parts of their own cultures and their own identity. I think success is based on the identity of the individual. As soon as schools try to trample down this sense of identity and try to create more uniformity — which they do most of the time — the student loses the ability to stand out and be that person that is successful. Making sure that the students are more in touch with who they are is fundamental in empowering them to be more successful people, so in that sense allowing these small things, these small leeways such as making sure that they speak their own languages in classes is a building-up effect to making sure that the student does come out as a successful student. Which is what the school wants."

Olerato, **Former Learner**

3

BATTLING
BIAS

Transformation in schools needs to begin with us looking inward at ourselves and our identity. That's where we need to start transforming. We need to begin to reflect on who we are as the adults in the school. How do we see ourselves and the world? How do we see others? How might this be shaping how we react to what is happening around us and how we react to what the young people in our schools are trying to tell us? Perhaps, if we can begin to take the time to listen to ourselves and understand what we think and how we react, we can begin to really listen to and understand the young people in our classrooms.

"I think personal bias is one of the biggest stumbling blocks to achieving trustful and trustworthy relationships between the pupil body and the teacher body. My experience in the context of where I teach is that the majority of teachers tend to defensively say, 'I'm not racist, I'm not biased, I've done nothing wrong.' They come from that position of almost entitlement, where they say, 'I'm the teacher. I'm the authority figure. I don't need to change because I've done nothing wrong.'"

Sue, **Teacher**

IT BEGINS WITH YOU

We sometimes forget that transformation, diversity, inclusivity and belonging are about people. While we do need structural changes in schools, such as new codes of conduct and new hiring and admissions policies, these visible aspects of transformation are driven by people – people who can just as easily reverse and stall as they can move forward. But it is often to the codes of conduct and admissions policies that we first turn because it's a lot easier to change words than it is to begin to shift what people believe, how they see themselves and how they see and treat one another.

Given that the codes of conduct, admissions and hiring policies, and the curriculum that is taught in classrooms is created, not by the young people in schools, but by the adults, it is with us that the process of transformation needs to begin. And by us, we mean the teachers, management and other adults working in schools. We need to reflect on who we are as role models in the school. How do we see ourselves and the world? How do we see others? How might this be shaping how we react to what is happening around us and how we react to what learners are trying to tell us? Perhaps, if we can begin to take the time to listen to ourselves and understand what we think and how we react, we can begin to really listen to and understand the young people in our classrooms.

Some of the best teachers and school leaders we have met are in part great because they are on a continual journey to learn more about themselves. They reflect on their practice, behaviours, their thinking, and their actions often. If one of our common goals as educators is to help young people become themselves and walk more comfortably and confidently in their own skin, then we need to be working towards self-awareness too. If we are not, it is less likely that we will consciously be helping learners to do this.

How we see ourselves impacts on how we see others and how we treat them. We too were adolescents once asking, "Who am I?" As adults, though, we find it more difficult to find the time or reasons to keep revisiting this question. Life, and especially schools, keep us very busy. But the more aware we are of the various aspects that make us who we are – our interests, religion, beliefs, and values – the more we open up the possibility to see others, our colleagues and learners, as more than just one trait, label or stereotype. As humans, we naturally label things and people in order to make sense of the world. But deeply understanding our own identity helps us to see beyond these labels to what makes each person unique. If I am able to see that I am more than a gender, race or nationality, I am more able to recognise this in you.

Self-awareness is more than an understanding of our own biases, however. It includes being sensitive to how we occupy our positions of power, and the unconscious impact we have on learners in how we acknowledge their presence. John Amaechi explains this well:

> To create an inclusive and emotionally literate environment, I think we also have to change the way that we think about our interactions …
>
> One of the markers of environments that are inclusive and emotionally literate is … that people with power accept, respect, understand their status and power. There's a lot of places where in an attempt to be closer to the kids, "down with the kids," adults in the environment, people with power, faculty members and principals kind of pretend that they

don't have this massive sway. And you just can't afford to do that. I think people with power need to start to think about/ of themselves like giants. They need to start to think about themselves the same way I think about myself in almost every environment. [John Amaechi weighed 128 kilograms at the peak of his career as a professional basketball player, and is 2.08 metres tall.]

I treat the world like it is made of cardboard in order to make sure that I don't accidently tear it at any stage. I think about that every time I go to open a door, so I don't swing it open off its hinges. I think about it in every space where I am around people. I am constantly checking my wing mirrors to make sure that nobody is in my space. So that I don't turn too quickly or stick my arm out or do whatever else that might decapitate a small person in my circumference. And I think that is a metaphor for how principals, faculty members, teachers, staff need to think about themselves. Because there is a kid in your school who looks at you and when they look up at you it is as if you are ten feet tall. And your merest gaze, your casual look in their direction, can have an impact on how they feel about themselves. Even if you are cross with a teacher that you've spoken with three minutes earlier, if you bring that irritation into a look as you walk through the hallways, they will think it is them and the impact on them will be huge because you are a huge figure in their lives.

"And I think a lot of people ... try and escape from the responsibility of their power by pretending that they don't have any."

And I think a lot of people ... try and escape from the responsibility of their power by pretending that they don't have any. And there is nothing more dangerous than a powerful person who doesn't believe they are. Not because of what they do intentionally, but because of the accidental damage you do when you don't realise you're a giant. And that's why I try to encourage people to imagine that in their hallways they are that giant. They can either be the very careful, very thoughtful, benevolent giant, or they can be the very clumsy one who decapitates kids on a daily basis without even knowing it.

I don't think that powerful people in schools – the teachers, the faculty, the staff, and the principals – I don't think they recognise how moving it is for a young person to be prioritised by attention. Just simply to be important enough to have and hold your full attention for a moment. I mean … this is one of those amazing things. I have a community centre in Manchester, and whilst I recognise that it's important and I try to be there all the time, I don't think I'd ever reversed this and thought about the impact on the young people. Until we had a kid, newly come into my centre and … very excited to talk to me – most of the people who are already at my centre [become] less excited over time … And he's talking to me and my phone goes off in my pocket. And he starts to turn away … automatically. And I just fumble with my phone in my pocket and press it on mute. And the kid just looks me in the face and then runs away crying.

What kind of world are we in where a kid's cue for exit is that a call comes in? And it doesn't matter if you're talking about nonsense or something of great gravity. Since when is a young person in your presence less important than a phone call? And then the other side of this – the weeping as he runs away. I asked [him] about it later on. He calmed down a bit, I brought him back. He was like, "Oh, well you know, I just assume that you'd have something better to do." We've got kids in every school in every city of almost every country that

I've ever visited who believe that they're less important than a person's attention for three minutes. That is something we can address by making sure that we're present in a school. And that is something I think that can have a massive impact on both the young people and the school environment in general.[3]

The starting point we want to put on the page is with you. While transforming schools and creating inclusive environments needs systemic interventions, involves policies, numbers and quotas, the hard work, the most important work, is working on ourselves. The policies won't really change until we do. Until we can listen to ourselves, we can't really listen to others. Until we are aware of the impact we have on young people, the sometimes-unconscious impact, we will never really allow our classrooms and schools to change. We have to be willing to set aside the time, expect it won't be easy, and be open to being honest with others, but most importantly, with ourselves. If we don't see transformation as something that begins with each one of us, then we will never really find ourselves in authentically transformed and inclusive schools.

---

3 "John Amaechi Discusses Identity", interview with Facing History and Ourselves.

"To me the most important education that takes place in schools is not the content of what I'm trying to teach you and it's not necessarily what happens in my classroom; it's the engagement that I have with you on the sports field, it's the engagement that I have with you in the corridors, the engagement of watching you, listening to you sing in the choir and chatting to you afterwards. It's my talking to you about something you read in the newspaper and you come to me and say to me, 'I didn't like what I read in the newspaper, what do you think?' and for us to have that kind of conversation. To me that is where education takes place.

I think it's critical, the role that a teacher plays, and teachers often have more influence on young teenagers than parents do. [Learners] probably spend more time at school than at home in their 12 years of schooling … The influence works both ways. So a teacher can make a remark about a child that is demeaning and belittling and the child will be severely affected by that in a negative way. But similarly, you can have a teacher who notices a child and says, 'I see that you've been looking a bit sad over the last couple of days, what can I do to help you?' The care that someone shows as a teacher in that particular moment will never be forgotten by that child. So the influence of teachers on children can never be underestimated. That is why as teachers we have to watch what we say and watch how we act. If we say things like 'Rugby is better than hockey' or use phrases, terrible phrases like 'You play mofstok' [an Afrikaans term for hockey that literally translates as 'gay stick' or 'gay hockey'] … [those are] derogatory and demeaning phrases … meant to illicit humour.

That's one of the things I often say to staff, 'You must be careful in trying to be funny that you don't offend. Because some of the jocks, let's say, in your class might be on your side and they might be laughing along with you. But there might be one little child who is sitting in the back in the corner who is nervously laughing along because that's what everyone else is doing. But inside, man, he's not happy."

Tony, **Principal**

US AND THEM

Everyone wants to belong. Everyone feels the natural need to be seen, heard and valued within a group. "Human beings," Professor Kwame Anthony Appiah reminds us, "are deeply and profoundly social. We are profoundly dependent on our interactions with one another just to become a person at all."[4]

Studies show that when we are a part of a group, when we are an "insider", we feel pride and have greater self-esteem. This increases as the status of our group improves, especially if we consider our group superior to others. We are drawn to being part of an In Group, while we see others as part of Out Groups.

In order to simplify sensory information and make sense of our world, our brains group and categorise things in a natural stereotyping process. We do this with people as well, putting them into In and Out Groups.

Our brains also exaggerate the differences between these groups. Let's say you are part of a group of young teachers who always sit together in the staffroom. This is your In Group. On the other side of the room is a group of older teachers who also always sit together. This is your Out Group. Your brain will exaggerate whatever differences you see between your In and Out groups to help you feel prouder and

---

4 Facing History and Ourselves, "Creating 'We and They': Kwame Anthony Appiah", interview with Facing History and Ourselves (Undated). Available at: https://www. facinghistory.org/resource-library/video/creating-we-and-they-kwame-anthony-appiah (accessed 20 April 2018)

more confident. The Out Group might appear much older and less fun than they actually are. At the same time, your brain exaggerates the positives of your In Group. Your colleagues might, for example, seem more humorous than they actually are.

This has consequences. In his book, *The Value of Difference: Eliminating Bias in the Workplace*, Professor Binna Kandola summarises what numerous psychological studies have shown when it comes to how we see our In and Out Groups. When we feel part of an In Group, we see the members as individuals. We might remember their names, notice and value individual characteristics, and form friendships easier. Where there are differences in this group (as there always are with human beings), we accept them. We will remember the positive things about, and interactions with, our In Group members. We will recall individual contributions, work harder for each other, and be prepared to make sacrifices for the group.

... to simplify sensory information and make sense of our world, our brains group and categorise things in a natural stereotyping process.

However, when we look at our Out Group, we see everyone not as individuals but as the same. We will remember more negative information about them. We will forget individual contributions, fail to put in as much effort for each other, and be reluctant to offer our support.

As Kandola goes on to show, being amongst our In Group invokes feelings of trust, worth, self-esteem and security, while being with our Out Group invokes feelings of anxiety, distrust, unfamiliarity, and hostility.[5]

It makes sense why we find it so hard to reach over to *them*. The natural need to belong to an In Group can quickly, easily and unconsciously become something that feels a little like prejudice and

---

5 Kandola, B (2009), *The Value of Difference: Eliminating Bias in the Workplace*, Kidlington: Pearn Kandola Publishing

discrimination towards others. Soon, we can find ourselves not only feeling distrust towards our Out Group, but also acting in unfair and harmful ways.

As teachers and leaders in schools, we need to recognise that some learners are a part of our In Group and others are part of our Out Group. Countless studies tell us that teachers are more likely to have lower expectations of Out Group students and remember what they did wrong and the times they misbehaved. As teachers in South African schools today, where our playgrounds, classrooms and staffrooms are divided between In and Out Groups, we have to remember that our brains, if left unchecked, will end up favouring *us* over *them*. While we will see some learners (and teachers) as individuals and remember their names and the good things they contribute, there will be others we will find it more difficult to support and work hard for. We will remember more of what they did wrong, and see them as somewhat hostile and, probably, distrustful.

In order to create truly transformed schools, where all feel they belong, we need to begin to counteract what our brains are naturally doing, push against those uncomfortable, anxious feelings and reach across to those in our Out Group.

"There was a time when this white student had walked in and she was late for class. So she got reprimanded … and … sat down. Then I walked in with a group of my friends, two or three of them. We walked in straight after, literally I could see that girl enter the class as I was going in. And we had to go back to our previous teacher and get a letter saying that we had just come from that class and the class ended later than it did. Yet a girl had just stepped in before us and she was just reprimanded and she sat down. She didn't have to go fetch the letter and stuff. And the interval between us walking in and her walking in was ten seconds max because I was able to hear the comments that were said to her. But we had to get proof that we didn't take our time walking from the previous class.

I think it's also a thing of how you can walk into a room and automatically you find someone more appealing than someone else. So as a black person, for example, if two people walk in chances are I'll pay more attention to the black person than the white person. So I think to a certain extent that went further. Some teachers weren't able to separate that 'Okay, I am fond of this child, but she's still going to get reprimanded as much as the other child that I'm not so fond of'.

It may be a coincidence. I can't say as a firm statement that it was a racial thing. It may just so happen that the naughty children happened to be black in that case. But at the end of the day all of our teachers were white, we only had one teacher who was black, so it's always going to seem like a racial thing even when it's not.

I think it was very unconscious, a lot of it, because the general stereotype is [that] a black boy from the township is aggressive or dangerous, more dangerous than a white kid from a suburban area with a good family. So most of the cases where you'd find a teacher has to approach a group of black kids, for example, he will be more stern, he'll be more aggressive for lack of a better word. Like he will approach that situation with more force than he would to a group of white boys, for example, because I think subconsciously he is entering a territory where the people are more aggressive, where the kids won't respond to you talking to them like normal humans, kind of thing. So I think it's that stereotype, that just because you come from a township you are rowdy, or you are dangerous or you are aggressive, those kind of things.

So I think it [was] those little things that came into play. Because you even saw it in the same race. Because I was considered the more 'white' black person, I would be given softer treatment. But if another black girl had done the exact same thing, just because she's from a township and she's maybe more outspoken or what, she would be handled in a more aggressive manner. So I think it's just those subconscious things that tap in and then the way they behave is just different towards different people."

Angelique, **Former Learner**

UNCONSCIOUS BIAS

There is no doubt that there are openly racist teachers at schools all over the country. Social media tends to bring them out.

But there are equally many teachers who would be offended to be accused of being racist or prejudiced. These teachers believe themselves to be colour-blind. We hear it often, "I don't see colour. We are all one race, the human race."

While the latter is true and science has proven that there is only one biological race, unfortunately society still has to catch up. And as far as our brain is concerned, we do see colour. For many of these teachers, who wouldn't consciously be prejudiced, it may come as a surprise, perhaps an uncomfortable realisation, that most of our prejudices occur without us even being aware of them.

Picture a prejudiced person. What kinds of things do they say? How do they behave? You are not like them, because you don't utter those words or behave the way they do. You cannot be prejudiced. Or so you tell yourself. This is what the conscious part of your brain tells you – that part you can hear and control, that "doesn't see colour". Unfortunately, the unconscious side of your brain thinks differently.

Only 2% of our emotional cognition happens consciously. This means that our biases – those feelings of trust and mistrust, and belonging and anxiety, that emerge when we are confronted by our In and Out Groups – emerge almost completely unconsciously.

Research has shown that while we may consciously believe and state that we are not biased against certain groups of people, our biases are evident in our actions. Neuroscientists have been able to support this research and observe what happens in the brain when we encounter difference and display bias. They have discovered that we respond to difference with the same part of the brain that responds to fear – the amygdala, a small set of neurons that makes associations between experiences and feelings quickly and automatically.

For example, if you eat something that makes you sick, the amygdala remembers the unpleasantness that follows those mouthfuls. If someone offers you that food in future, you will probably turn it down without consciously thinking about it. Similarly, the amygdala processes our interactions with people. If you were raised in a society that, for instance, valued your race more than others, chances are the amygdala has absorbed those messages and experiences and has stored associations between people, skin colour, and their perceived value. So, even if your conscious brain tells you that you don't see race or you don't think those of a different skin colour are any less than you, you might, for instance, find yourself, instinctively, clutching your bag a little tighter when someone of a different race walks by.

This doesn't mean we are all naturally racist, sexist, homophobic or xenophobic. It means that our brain is harbouring prejudices against some people that we aren't aware of. But to the person walking past on the pavement, our unconscious clutching might make us appear racist to them.

These unintentional behaviours can have an impact. The person walking past will start to pick up on what are called microaggressions – subtle, often unconscious, automatic and unintentional behaviours that send out negative messages to those who are receiving them. The message to the passerby on the pavement is that they are untrustworthy. Over time, and through constant

They have discovered that we respond to difference with the same part of the brain that responds to fear.

exposure to microaggressions, the recipients of these messages can begin to feel unwelcome.

This has important implications for education. In all schools, there are young people who are in a minority or who are not part of the dominant culture. While teachers may be trying their best not to see differences, their unconscious biases might be impacting on marginalised learners.

Because this happens unconsciously, it's easy to feel that there is very little we can do about it. But there is a way for us to become aware of our implicit biases.

A test developed by scientists at Harvard University, called the Implicit Association Test (IAT), monitors the unconscious associations we make between images (white and black faces if you take the "Race" test) and positive and negative emotions. The results indicate the degree to which we hold specific unconscious biases. Millions of people around the world have taken the anonymous tests on age, gender, race and sexuality, among other, biases. You can take the IAT online at https://implicit.harvard.edu. The aggregated results of the "Race" test are interesting. The majority of white respondents "show a preference for white over black" and half of black respondents show "a pro-white bias".[6] This does not mean that the majority of white people are racist. But it does mean that the majority of white respondents and half of black respondents harbour biases against black people that they were most likely unaware of.

The first step in gaining some control over what seems uncontrollable is awareness. Having just read this and knowing that you have implicit biases that are likely having an impact on people you interact with, you now need to take the IAT. While the test is not perfect and is worth taking a few times, short of climbing into a MRI scanner, this is the only

---

6 "'Project Implicit FAQs", https://implicit.harvard.edu/implicit/demo/background/faqs.html#faq7 (accessed 14 February 2018)

way we can currently get some idea of the unconscious biases we hold.

Share the outcome with colleagues and talk about some of the things you can do to begin to get the conscious part of your brain to take some control over your unconscious thinking. In the "Where to begin" chapter, on page 145, we have listed some practical steps to take in unlearning our unconscious behaviour.

The challenge then is to push against what biology naturally wants us to do and question why we feel certain emotions towards others or behave differently in their presence. If we just ignore what our brain is unconsciously doing, we are being lazy. It takes work to counteract the quick assumptions our brain makes about people, to uncover the unconscious biases we hold, and to begin to deal with these.

"I am thinking about unconscious bias a lot. I would be foolish to suggest that I don't have any biases myself. I'm quite clear on the fact that having grown up in apartheid South Africa, having had mostly white friends and white associates, that this idea of seeing the world through white eyes has to be there.

You know, it comes up. Not so much in a sense of race, though I'm sure there is racial bias there as well – but it comes up in a sort of an economic bias to some extent, in the implicit expectation of the boys in our school. For instance, the expectation that they will be at school at a particular time, they will play sport, and they will leave sport at a particular time, and then they will go home, they will do their homework, and all those kinds of things. I think what we've had to start realising is that's not the world that most, or many of our kids, live in. Particularly as we have more township kids coming to the school, that for them the morning begins incredibly early in order to catch transport to get to school. That to make it to a sports game, to a sports match, to a sports practice is actually quite challenging at times. And then to get home in time to do homework in an environment where perhaps homework isn't that easy to do, you know. Those kinds of things are becoming quite clear and we sort of have to shift our view, shift our understanding of how we collect these people from disparate and different backgrounds in one place and we have the same expectation for all of them.

Now, whether that's right or wrong I'm not entirely sure at this point. This is something we're battling with and coming to an understanding of — how we can deal differently with, or allow for differences and still seem to be fair in that regard."

Shaun, **Principal**

4

SEEKING DIFFERENCE

The challenge to school leaders is to seek out difference – to push against the human attraction to sameness and the comfort of familiarity. School leaders need to deliberately create more diverse staffrooms and classrooms, not only because learners need to be able to navigate through and succeed in a multi-cultural and diverse world, but also because it is morally right to do so.

"I think at least part of the problem of why these schools are struggling to transform adequately is because private schools, and to an extent Model-C schools as well, see themselves as islands. They see themselves as existing independently somehow from the rest of the educational system and the rest of South Africa, and don't see themselves as being beholden to the needs of South Africa more broadly."

Markus, **Former Learner**

DEALING WITH DIFFERENCE

In his poem, "What Do We Do with a Variation?", James Berry reflects on how we generally respond when confronted with difference.

What do we do with a difference?
Do we stand and discuss its oddity
or do we ignore it?

Do we shut our eyes to it
or poke it with a stick?
Do we clobber it to death?

Do we move around it in rage
and enlist the rage of others?
Do we will it to go away?

Do we look at it in awe
or purely in wonderment?
Do we work for it to disappear?

Do we pass it stealthily
or change route away from it?
Do we will it to become like ourselves?

What do we do with a difference?
Do we communicate to it,
let application acknowledge it
for barriers to fall down?[7]

7 Berry, J (2004), "What Do We Do with a Variation?," in *Only One of Me: Selected Poems*, London: Macmillan Children's Books.

Berry wasn't writing about transformation in South African schools, but barring "clobbering it to death", he may as well have been.

Our efforts to transform and integrate schools haven't been good enough. In many schools, racial demographics of learners don't reflect a country that has been, for more than 20 years, democratic, free and in the eyes of the law, non-racial. In those schools where racial demographics are more representative, learners past and present tell us that even when it looks like our schools are diverse, how we are dealing with difference – from "ignoring it" to "willing it to become like ourselves" – isn't working.

There is a lack of diversity in most staffrooms, too. Somewhere in the process of advertising posts, sifting through CVs, and eventually interviewing potential new teachers, it seems, as Berry suggests, we have worked difference to "disappear", and perhaps we have "changed route away from it". Most principals interviewing candidates who are of a different race and who have taught at poorer schools would not be able to say they really "communicated to" or "let application acknowledge" difference "for barriers to fall down". We haven't done well with variations.

In order for schools to transform, we have to go against our natural inclination to seek out those who look like us and who share our views, values, and priorities.

The challenge to school leaders is to seek out difference – to push against the human attraction to sameness and the comfort of familiarity. School leaders need to deliberately create more diverse staffrooms and classrooms, not only because learners need to be able to navigate through and succeed in a multi-cultural and diverse world, but also because it is morally right to do so.

There has been very little recent research in South Africa on the impact of a lack of diversity in staffrooms on learners in the classroom. But studies in the United States show that learners of colour benefit when they are taught by teachers who look like them.

Leading education expert, Gloria Ladson-Billings, describes a situation that is very familiar to many South African learners:

> I do know the experience of walking into schools (especially elementary and middle schools) where Black students ask me with eagerness, "Are you a teacher here?" And I recognize the disappointment that falls over those same faces when I shake my head, "No." Their longing for a teacher that "looks like them" is palpable. The current statistics indicate that class after class of children – Black, Native American, Latino, and Asian – go through entire school careers without ever having a teacher of their same race or ethnicity …[8]

Findings of research conducted in the United States explain why it is that Ladson-Billings recognises the disappointment on the faces of the black and brown students she meets. Studies have found that when black and brown learners are taught by teachers of their own colour, their maths and reading scores improve. In contrast, this has a neutral impact on the performance of white students. Studies have also found that white teachers will generally hold lower expectations of the black and brown learners in their classrooms.[9]

While the United States education system is very different to South Africa's as a whole, the issues that learners of colour face there mirror those in former Model-C and private schools here. In many of

8 "Ladson-Billings examines, 'What if we had more black teachers?'", University of Wisconsin-Madison, https://www.education.wisc.edu/soe/news-events/news/2015/01/19/ladson-billings-examines---what-if-we-had-more-black-teachers- (accessed 2 February 2018)

9 Binkovitz, L (24 April 2017), "Why Black and Brown Students need Black and Brown Teachers", *Houston Chronicle*. Available at https://www.houstonchronicle.com/local/gray-matters/article/Why-black-and-brown-students-need-black-and-brown-11089875.php (accessed 26 April 2018).

these schools, children of colour are in a minority (demographically or culturally). There are learners in former Model-C schools and private schools who, like their American counterparts, never see someone who looks like them standing in front of the classroom, let alone leading the school. What they do see is many white teachers standing in front of the classroom who might, like their American counterparts, be holding lower expectations of them.

It wasn't just concerning to Ladson-Billings that the majority of black learners would never be taught by black teachers and that they are disadvantaged in a system that holds lower expectations of them. Her attention was also drawn to the white learners in these classrooms and the impact that a lack of diversity in the staffrooms has on them:

> I want to suggest that there is something that may be even more important than Black students having Black teachers and that is White students having Black teachers! It is important for White students to encounter Black people who are knowledgeable and hold some level of authority over them. Black students ALREADY know that Black people have a wide range of capabilities. They see them in their homes, their neighborhoods, and their churches. They are the Sunday School teachers, their Scout Leaders, their coaches, and family members. But what opportunities do White students have to see and experience Black competence?[10]

In many South African schools, white students are taught by white teachers. They only encounter adults of colour on the school premises

---

10 "Ladson-Billings examines, 'What if we had more black teachers?'", University of Wisconsin-Madison, https://www.education.wisc.edu/soe/news-events/news/2015/01/19/ladson-billings-examines---what-if-we-had-more-black-teachers- (accessed 2 February 2018)

who are employed as cleaning and maintenance staff. Black learners, on the other hand, encounter black adults "who are knowledgeable and hold some level of authority over them" on a daily basis. It would be reasonable to expect that when white learners leave school, the very idea of black competence will be unfamiliar to them. At a minimum, we can expect an unconscious bias that favours and respects lighter over darker skins. At worse, these biases will be very real and conscious and accepted.

Of course, we cannot simply transfer research findings from American schools onto our schools. More research needs to be conducted on South African schools around the impact of teacher diversity. But in the absence of this, and given the similarities in the demographics and experiences between American and some South African schools, perhaps we can approach these research findings with "could" in mind. What if we looked at our former Model-C and private schools and asked, "Could the black learners in our schools thrive here if they had the opportunity to be taught by more black teachers? Could the white learners thrive if they were able to see more black teachers in authority, more black adults who are knowledgeable and capable? Could some of our teachers be holding lower expectations of the black learners in their classrooms?"

We have nothing to lose by assuming that some of what has been found across our shores could be happening here. Without transformed staffrooms that allow all learners the opportunity to be taught by teachers who look like them and teachers who don't look like them, we are not only continuing to disadvantage some of our learners, but we are also not adequately preparing all of our learners to thrive in a diverse and changing society and workplace when they leave school.

Even though we live in a diverse country that offers so much possibility of bringing difference into our staffrooms, we cannot afford, as James Berry's poem reminds us, to still "pass it stealthily" any longer. We need to ask deliberately, "How could we deal with difference differently in our school and especially in our staffrooms? How could difference make our schools thrive?"

"I remember interviewing and then actually hiring a particular teacher. She was quite a small lady, young at the time, and from a very tough background herself … She was a language teacher who had a real passion for her language and creative writing, poetry especially. And I remember in the interview just finding out about her, and it was very clear that her background matched and was very similar to many of the pupils at our school — tough circumstances, a lot of changes at home, not an amazing school environment, rising out of that because of her own commitment and work ethic.

Fairly recently actually she led a devotion in assembly where she shared quite deeply about some of those aspects of her life, some of the struggles in her life, which she hadn't done before. She'd probably been at our school for two or three years, and she actually mentioned in the devotion, she said, 'I consciously haven't spoken about some of these things because it makes me a bit vulnerable. But I kind of feel I'm ready to.' And she read one or two of her poems, which were about those environments, and her journey and of overcoming them, and some of the really good things in those environments.

That was actually her message, that people see the gangsterism and they see the teenage pregnancies but they don't see the other side. And you could just feel amongst the pupil body, you could feel the resonance with people who knew that environment, who lived in similar environments and maybe hadn't really been able to bring that into our school environment. They felt that everybody at our school was a bit more together and their lives were fine, and they didn't have those same struggles, and 'I don't think I could talk about that kind of stuff at school'. And this teacher doing it really opened up that space and made it possible. And she spoke a lot in what she would call Kaapse Afrikaans [Cape Afrikaans], sort of slang, coloured slang from the Cape Flats. And some identified with it fully who know those environments and who know the language. A big section of the school would be isiXhosa-speaking and wouldn't understand that, but that wasn't a barrier. They could understand the sense of it, they could understand the message in it; people could translate for them from nearby and so on. The heart of the message was certainly important and felt by all."

Murray, **Principal**

HIRING FOR DIFFERENCE

Given the very slow pace of transformation in staffrooms across the country, and the growing political language of race, increasing pressure will be placed on schools, especially former Model-C and private schools, to change what their teachers look like and where they come from. At some point, this will be an issue that voters take to the polls.

Unlike in business and sport, where clear targets for transformation are set by government, schools have not had as much pressure and incentives to authentically transform. In schools that can afford to hire staff beyond what the state provides, and that have the finances and flexibility to hire with race in mind, there has been surprisingly little transformation of staff.

Schools have a choice to wait until they are forced to radically transform, or to begin to do so now, to shape the transformation, to strengthen it and to allow the changes to make them even more successful.

School leaders need to begin to hire staff with difference as a priority and deliberately begin to build a team of teachers that complements each other instead of one that is uniform, looks the same and speaks the same language. Principals need to be looking at different personalities, different ways of viewing the world, and in the complexity of South Africa, different cultural perspectives, backgrounds and social classes.

It is so easy to do what comes naturally – for principals to re-invent themselves, their current team of teachers and the history of those who have walked the hallways before. The bias of every interviewer is to look for people who are like them – unless they are trained to look for something different. Often, those who conduct interviews to hire new teachers – principals, deputies, and sometimes governing body members – have no formal training in staff recruitment, let alone how to overcome their implicit biases. Given their inclination to hire staff who are more like them, the composition of the interviewing team needs to reflect the racial and cultural diversity the school is seeking. They need to reflect difference, understand difference, and look for different things.

When a candidate from a township school applies for a position at your school, do you assume that all township schools are poorly run and badly managed, and that therefore the teacher who comes from there won't fit into the culture of your school? Do we have the tools to evaluate what success looks like at those schools as opposed to what success looks like at former Model-C and private schools? Do you seek out and build connections with principals who you don't traditionally meet with so that you can ask questions? Do you understand how that school operates, or how that person operates within that particular school environment? The interviewing team needs to equip itself with the necessary skills to look beyond what they know and the composition of their current staff.

Governing bodies also need to be more deliberate in hiring principals of colour. Being deliberate means changing what you think you are looking for. In a recent advertisement for a principal of a public boys' school, amongst the qualities and qualifications they listed was that candidates needed to show "proven success in a similar environment of high achievement in academics, culture and sport" and should have "at least five years' [experience] as Principal/ Headmaster (preferable), or Deputy in a boys'

> *Being deliberate means changing what you think you are looking for.*

high school (preferable)". If this school was serious about wanting to transform the leadership of their school and open the door to hiring a principal of colour, those two sentences severely limit that possibility. There are currently only a handful, a very small handful, of people of colour who have taught or occupied leadership positions in "similar environments of high achievement in academics, culture and sport" – in other words, a former Model-C or private school, and in this case, a boys' school, where even fewer principals or deputy principals of colour can be found. Of course, nowhere in the advertisement does it mention anything about looking for a principal of colour. It's unlikely they had a diverse range of applications and even less likely that they now have a principal of colour.

How do we break the almost incestuous cycle of swopping principals and staff at former Model-C and private schools? Because we look for people who have attended or taught at these schools, we end up hiring white middle-class teachers and principals over and over again with the argument, "Well, they were the best candidates."

"Best" from whose perspective? "Best" in this context is not an objective measurement; it is a subjective assessment made by someone who is unaware of the psychological dynamics that unfold in the staff-recruitment process.

We need to set out to *not* hire a teacher from a school that looks just like ours. We need to stop expecting that candidates for positions in our school must have experience at schools like ours. It is about breaking that expectation and breaking assumptions.

"I think you will find that many schools have different ideas of what a successful teacher is. Really, if we came down to the nitty-gritty, we should all believe that a successful teacher is the person who is getting through to the child in the classroom because education is our core business. But I think very often it's dollied up by, 'Are they good at a sport, are they good at one of the extramurals that you offer?' And I think it is for people in my position to actually take that step back and say, 'Who is going to be successful and where do you look at success?' Success isn't always about getting the top mark in matric. For me success is always having a girl, particularly a girl that wasn't coping in grade 8, leave at Valedictory and I know that she can go out into the world and she can cope. That is done by the teachers in the classroom.

I think one of the things that has happened to me over the last couple of years is I read CVs differently. I do look for people of colour. I don't just discard. I do read through every testimonial that is given and every CV that's given. My own journey has made me realise that I might have been overlooking good people. It's an interesting thing because, yes definitely, one used to be prejudiced and go, 'They haven't got the experience of one of the big schools, they haven't got the experience of this kind of school.' And then it makes you sit back and say, 'Well, what is this kind of school? What is so special about this kind of school?' Maybe we need to be more open.

It crept in gradually as I realised that I needed to actively look for people of colour in my staffroom, that there was a commitment to it. I think years before it was a case of, 'Yes, we should if they're great.' What I termed great I'm not sure that I actually had quantified for myself, but I am quite sure now that I left out people who would have been fantastic.

So there's a lot to be said about the fact [that] we've got to look at people differently. It's not the bells and whistles. What they have managed? The kind of marks that they are getting with their matrics, or their grade 10s or whatever, with the little resources [they have] is far in excess [of] any of my teachers, maybe, who are getting the same marks, maybe slightly better, but with millions more resources. And you need to actually say, 'Well, that teacher, given the resources, is going to just fly.' So maybe reading the CVs a lot better … And I found that I have.

But since I've made this commitment I definitely look at people differently and I look actively for something that could enhance my school. Maybe I don't offer it now, maybe they do have an extramural that's fantastic. I don't offer it, but maybe I could and maybe that would be a wider diversity to offer the girls that I have."

Shirley, **Principal**

MENTORING AND CHAMPIONING

In order to change the demographics of our staff we have to change our approach. If we wait on the slow process of attrition of staff – of people leaving, dying, or retiring – before we replace them with more representative teachers and school leaders, we will wait too long, and society will become increasingly impatient.

We need to mentor current staff from minority groups who have shown promise. But we also need to champion them.

Mentoring is taking someone under your wing, teaching them skills, and showing them what to do and when to do it. Often mentoring is done without an actual plan or career path in mind for the mentee so that they can eventually be promoted within the organisation.

Championing is identifying, developing, and supporting someone to a position within the school. As in any organisation, often, those who fit in with the dominant culture of the school, who thrive in it, and who are friends with those who have power in the school are championed into promotions and career opportunities. But we need to champion staff who don't represent the dominant culture of the school.

Co-author Roy Hellenberg describes how championing changed his career path at a school where we was in the minority as a teacher of colour:

> My experience at my previous school was a very positive one, of someone not only mentoring but championing me as an individual within the school structure.

I became good friends with Gary, one of the HODs at the school, because he was the superintendent of the boarding house and we had met in other environments before. I remember that he took me out for lunch one day. There was a position that was advertised for senior housemaster in the boarding house. It had briefly crossed my mind to apply, but I felt I had no experience. Certainly, boarding wasn't a part of my upbringing in my own family; not even in my broader community. Also, living on the campus, never having the opportunity to be away from school was not something that appealed to me at the time. Extra time at school wasn't what had made me a successful teacher at the previous schools I had taught at.

But I remember Gary inviting me for lunch and asking me if I had considered applying for the position. I gave him my reasons why I thought not to apply. But he actively encouraged me to apply. He told me he had watched me over the three years I had been at the school and that he had seen that I had all the individual components – the management ability, the consistency, the fairness, and the understanding of strategic planning that are absolutely necessary within a boarding establishment. He pointed out that my ability to work with parents, boys and staff, while individual and separate in me at the time, could be brought together within the boarding establishment. He said that what I lacked in the position, he would make sure I developed by guiding and mentoring me through the process. He spoke about how this position was an important stepping stone in my career path. One that I had not seen, having never been exposed to the culture of boarding and the strategic space the boarding house occupies in traditional boys' schools. I remember that conversation because it was a critical one that got me to think about a position within that school that I had not thought of before. I applied for the position and I was successful. I was the senior housemaster for seven years.

Looking back now, as I sit as deputy headmaster at a new school – another traditional boys' school – I understand what Gary was really doing for me. He was bringing together two critical skills. On the one side, teaching and sport involvement, which I already possessed. And on the other side, boarding experience. He knew that given that boarding houses are the backbones of traditional boys' schools, anyone who thinks of being in a leadership position in these schools will have to have some experience of that boarding culture.

[Gary's] decision to mentor and champion me so many years ago brought me to the school I am currently at. Certainly, they weren't looking for a head of History, and they weren't looking for a master in charge of rowing, which was what I did in academics and in sport. This school was looking for someone to turn their boarding house around. And I had that to offer.

When you have someone who understands the system and who champions your cause within the system, who understands the next steps you need to take in order to develop yourself and go forward, you have access and insight. These are hard to find when you are a teacher of colour in former Model-C and private schools. But this access and insight allow for good choices to be made that can see the promotion of black people within white-dominated leadership environments.

Of course, we still need to make sure that we follow fair labour practices and procedures. But it is possible to do both. It is done fairly and legally in the corporate world all the time. People are groomed, mentored, and championed to take up the next position. As long as the process remains fair and clear, and the person is judged on their ability and potential to do the job, we too can champion those in minorities in our schools.

"Sometimes … choosing to create a diverse staffing group [is] not always the easiest road. Sometimes there is a different person who would just be a smooth fit in the school, who's like the others, who thinks the same way and so on, but that's not necessarily the person who is going to be the most effective. So sometimes you make a different choice and it requires a bit more work; you've got to get alongside that person. They might have strengths of who they are, the language they speak, the environment they come from, but then there might be some other weaknesses. But those strengths are worth the extra work … maybe you need to work harder on classroom management or maybe their computer skills aren't as good – but [it's] an active decision to say [that] these other things – [the] other values that they're going to bring to our environment, the strengths – are worth it, are important."

Murray, **Principal**

REACHING OUT

The South African Schools Act gives learners the right to attend the school that is closest to where they live. In principle, this makes sense and ensures that each child has access to schools close to home and within their community.

But the complexity of post-apartheid South Africa is that while the laws no longer inhibit where we can live, economics still does. Many of the schools with better resources and facilities are situated in more affluent, former white suburbs. This means that children from families who can afford to live in those areas are given the right to attend these good schools. Poorer families can't get in. And schools can keep refusing young people who live too far away.

Unless a concerted effort is made to connect with different communities and change the demographics of the learner body, the system as it is will continue to allow schools to draw predominantly from the wealthy white families that surround them.

... we all have something to offer each other, to help each other grow, and to help each other to develop and become better.

When recruiting learners, if schools continue to advertise only to their traditional white, middle-class market, the demographics of the school won't change. The Bureau of Market Research has published findings that, on average, black male professionals earn only 30% of what white male professionals make, and black female professionals earn only 65% of what their white counterparts make.[11] We need to ask: Are we deliberately, or unintentionally, pricing ourselves out of the market that would ensure diversity by keeping our school fees so high that they are unaffordable for many black families? Or do we operate by an unspoken rule (or bias) to keep the ratio 70/30 – 70% white and 30% learners from other groups – so that "standards" and "discipline" can be maintained? These are difficult and uncomfortable questions to ask and conversations to be had. But ask and speak we must.

High school principals of former Model-C and private schools should connect with schools in townships and places where the demographics do not represent that of their own schools or neighbourhoods. Principals must identify township and other schools that succeed despite a lack of resources. They should investigate these schools and attend their sports days or other events. They must visit the principals of those schools to have conversations and ask to walk around and see how learning takes place. There are new, different and exciting feeder schools to be found if we start doing things differently.

Given that transformation will take time, we can also connect with and build partnerships with schools that are further along the transformation path than we are. These partnerships should take into account the strengths and weaknesses of both schools, so that the assets of each school flows into the deficits of the other. These are partnerships that don't presume that those who have fewer physical resources have nothing or little to offer. They presume that we all have something to offer each other, to help each other grow, and to help each other to develop and become better.

---

11 *BusinessTech* (13 July 2016), "Shocking Pay Difference Between Black and White Professionals in South Africa", https://businesstech.co.za/news/business/129980/shocking-difference-in-pay-between-black-and-white-professionals-in-sa/ (accessed 8 March 2018)

It takes time, effort and understanding to build equal partnerships. But these can build bridges and connections between young people. Young people overcome barriers very quickly when we provide them with the opportunity to do so, and schools have to take responsibility for that. Schools have to be decisive and clear in their strategy to create this multi-cultural world and to add value to it, especially when their demographics do not reflect this. Through connecting to difference, through partnerships with different schools, through relationships in different communities, through reaching out, difference can be brought in.

"If you're wanting to shift the culture of a school perhaps to a more open or a more democratic culture, a definite key step is opening up conversations within the school. It's wonderful if you can transform the people there and make it more representative, but even with a very unrepresentative group you can still work with topics, issues you know. What's going on in the country? If it's a fairly middle-, upper-class group themselves, what do they understand about what's happening out there? Have representatives come in and share and talk and debate. You can start opening up the experience, and that isn't a major change.

You're not throwing out important days, you're not not playing sport any more. You're adding a layer to what gets spoken about within the school. You can invite key guest speakers to come and present talks on various topics. You can choose what you are getting your pupils involved in, in the outings that they have. It could be to a different environment that they wouldn't have normally been exposed to – to a different faith environment, to visit a different church or a mosque or something that wouldn't be typical. Or go to a different area of your city that's less resourced or more poverty-ridden? Or through sports matches – do you only play sports matches against schools who are like you? It's tempting because those schools are well organised and they run a good programme and have the same number of teams as you. But the value to have your players, your young people, playing against a very different school and maybe going to their school that's not that well resourced, can open eyes a bit.

I think that a crucial part of this whole process is that you have to have different voices within the school. If we are moving, trying to be inclusive and open to different people, that's got to be represented by who gets to talk and who gets to articulate things within the school. Hopefully you have those voices available on your staff, within your pupil body. It often isn't balanced. Maybe you've got a lot more of one type of person in your school. But you can find representatives from other groups within the school, whether those are religious groups or race groups — it doesn't really matter — but to make sure at different times in assembly, or at your parents' meetings or at significant functions like a prize-giving or so on, that different people get a turn to articulate who they are and what's important to them. The pupils see that, and they need to see themselves reflected in who is up there, you know, which scriptures are read — are different faiths' scriptures included at different times?

It is important as well to look at the demographics of your institution, your intake of pupils. Places in schools are at a premium in our country. We know that people are desperate for good schools. But if this thing of transformation is important, then you need to reflect that in who's coming into your school. How deliberate are you? If along with your governing body you want to make changes, then set a five-year plan of how you're going to change those numbers."

Murray, **Principal**

5

LEADING
FOR CHANGE

In many respects, a principal's leadership is as, if not more important, than that of a national leader. Some will say this but not truly believe it. If they did, then they would understand that a school leader today cannot lead from her ego. She has to lead, is being called to lead, in a way that benefits the nation, the community, and most importantly, the young people she serves today, and those she will serve tomorrow.

"You'd battle to find a school adopting any kind of transformative journey if the head of that school didn't believe in it. Conversely, if you've got a head who believes passionately in it, the journey is a much easier one to take. So that sounds pretty obvious but if the leader of an organisation doesn't believe in the transformative journey, or the transformation journey, it's going to battle to happen."

Tony, **Principal**

BUILDING A COUNTRY

"We have a country to build, dammit!
We have a country to build!"

These were the loud, urgent and demanding words that got the few hundred school leaders and teachers we had brought together to sit up a little straighter. It would have been hard for anyone there that morning in a Midrand conference centre not to have found themselves returning to a memory of a childhood scolding from a parent or a loved one. The kind of scolding that, because it was delivered out of love, left you with an uncomfortable embarrassment and the need to do better next time, to be better.

That 2007 scolding was handed down by Denis Goldberg, Rivonia Trialist and one of South Africa's greatest elders.

It was 2017 when Seth Mazibuko, one of the leaders of the June 16 Soweto Uprisings, also stood in front of teachers and school leaders we invited to listen to him.

"Response. Ability. Responsibility."

His was less a scolding than an honest admission. "If you are a principal or a teacher and do not have the ability to respond," he told us, "then resign." Many of us found ourselves again sitting up a little straighter.

It was no coincidence that we had invited these particular leaders to begin a conversation with principals and teachers. Each could have made very different choices years before. One could have done what most white South Africans did during apartheid – very little. The other was 15 years old in 1976. Children should not find themselves having to throw stones to fight an unjust and repressive system. But each of them, at times when choices seemed more difficult and there were enough reasons to look away or retain the status quo, chose to bring about change.

In the ten years that have separated Denis and Seth's messages, it has been harder and harder to find visionary, selfless and compassionate leaders – in politics, business and even in schools. It has become difficult to find those leaders who help us still believe that we can be better than what we are, who inspire us to reach for something deep within ourselves that defines our humanity and brings it out in us. It is difficult to find those leaders who bring everyone in and then are able to walk along with them.

Yet we've experienced so many who have done this before, who have risen up and looked deep inside of themselves. In spite of their circumstances, in spite of their situations or what others may have done to them or thought of them, they refused to be turned into small-minded individuals intent on satisfying their needs alone. Their offering of selflessness resonated with something deep inside of us and we believed we could be better than we were. Nelson Mandela did that for us. Albertina Sisulu lifted and guided us. Ahmed Kathrada found courage again and again to speak up and speak for. Archbishop Desmond Tutu and Denis Goldberg still find their last bits of energy to bend the arc of the moral universe a little closer towards justice.

And people like Seth Mazibuko still rise above themselves to take us further than where we are today, to where we believe we can be.

These leaders were part of a political and social movement for change. Of course, while they were working to create a more just and fair country, many schools at the time were very good at protecting their learners from the changes occurring around them. For many white South Africans attending schools during apartheid, there was very little mention or engagement with what was happening outside the school grounds. White schools on the whole were very good at keeping change out. One could argue, many of these schools are still pretty good at this.

But change is upon us. The changes in society, from universities to the increasing poverty and alienation that face millions of South Africans, have arrived at the school gates. Young people are finding their voices very loudly on Facebook and WhatsApp. Technology has brought about shorter and shorter periods of social change. We are no longer dealing with an opportunity to change over the next 15 years. We are talking about the next three to five years. Generational theory now says that a generation of social change can be as short as two years.

Generational theory now says that a generation of social change can be as short as two years.

Yet in many schools we keep hearing that things need to stay the same. Many schools deal with change by keeping it out, holding onto a successful past and finding that to be a comfortable buffer, or at least a convenient pause button to keep what's happening outside from coming in. Somehow, past success causes them to believe that change is not necessary to succeed in the future.

Of course, there are foundations of education that will and should always remain solid. We will borrow from Nyerere, from Plato, from Frere, and others who have thought deeply about how one educates for life. These principles remain as a part of our foundational structure. But the superstructure that we build on top needs to look different today. Architects don't design the same buildings that their predecessors did 50 years ago. They draw on inspiration and lessons from the past, and there are building principles that remain, but skyscrapers wouldn't reach as high nor would buildings become as green if things stayed the same.

While architects build around the changing environment, we say that educators and leaders in education are often the last to change. Why is that so? Why do we tolerate this? Why are so many schools running along the same lines and operating along much the same principles as they did 50 years ago?

In many respects, a principal's leadership is as, if not more important, than that of a national leader. Some will say this but not truly believe it. If they did, then they would understand that a school leader today cannot lead from her ego. She has to lead, is being called to lead, in a way that benefits the nation, the community, and most importantly, the young people she serves today, and those she will serve tomorrow.

When Seth Mazibuko spoke to school leaders and teachers, he spoke of three ages that he had lived through – the Stone Ages, as he calls them. The first was the *Throwing Stones Age*, which began on June 16 as he picked up stones and led the student uprisings that followed. He was later arrested and sent to Robben Island, where he spent five years in the quarry – the *Breaking Stones Age*. The final stage, in which he is in now, is *Gathering Stones* – uniting South Africans and working to improve education. That, as he says, is his responsibility.

We have the ability to respond. We have the responsibility. We have a country to build, dammit!

Principals and teachers need to start gathering stones. It might be to place them down to step through gentle waters, or it might be to build a bridge to get over stronger currents. Either way, stones need to be collected. We have the ability to respond. We have the responsibility. We have a country to build, dammit!

"The principals are not just leading the staff and learners and that's it. There must be that vision of what it is that we are doing to build these kids who are going to go out there in the world and face the challenges that we have in our country and all sorts of things. It is very important for a principal to have that kind of a vision, to say, 'This is where we are as country, and in order to build a better country, what should we do? How do we best prepare our kids so that they go out there and make sure that they excel in whatever they do?'

So even the staff as well, I think they never had any problem because whatever I do, I involve them. Immediately when I arrived we had a sort of a conference where I indicated where the school wanted to go to, what we wanted to do with the school, where we were going. I got them involved in drawing up the 2020 vision for our school. The SMT [Senior Management Team] were also involved. So they felt, 'It's like he wants us, he wants to hear our voices as well.' It's not like it was a document that I set down myself and said, 'This is what is going to happen.' It involved everybody, including the SGB [School Governing Body], so that they should know the vision that we want to have.

And one of the things that I'm doing at the moment is involving the old boys, who I think were not actively involved. I think the reason why they were not actively involved is because of tradition. Maybe they felt it has changed because there are no longer white kids there. And I think, perhaps, they were not brought in to say, 'You still matter, we still want to listen to you, what is it that we can do to take the school forward?'

So I had the principal's breakfast where I had to call them and give them the vision of where the school is going and indicate to them that it is their school, and their voices matter. It doesn't mean that because there are many black kids here they can't be actively involved. So I'm bringing them on board. They've shown tremendous interest. I think they are beginning to have confidence in the school, to say they can be part of it.

One of the things, really, that I always preach to my boys, is to say our job really as staff, as educators, is not really to make them get As in Maths and English. It's for them to be excellent in whatever they do. One of the favourite quotes that I like is by Dr Martin Luther King Jr. who said, 'Whatever your life's work is, do it well. Even if it does not fall in the category of the so-called big professions, do it well. If it falls your lot to be a street sweeper, sweep streets like Shakespeare wrote poetry, like Michelangelo painted pictures, like Beethoven composed music. Sweep streets so well up until the host of heaven will have to pause and say, "Here lived a great street sweeper who swept his job so well."'

My point really is that we need to inculcate the spirit of excellence in our kids but still [be] looking at the challenges that we are facing as a country. What is it that we can do better? A visionary leader is needed not only for our kids to do well academically, but also to show how they become better citizens when they leave the school and go beyond into the world."

Meneer, **Principal**

RETHINKING POLICIES

Netflix's "Expensing, Entertainment, Gifts and Travel Policy", which guides how the leadership and employees at the online streaming company spend its money at the office, when travelling for work, or entertaining clients, reads:

Act in Netflix's best interests.

That's it, the wording of the policy in its entirety.

That's one word less than the actual name of the policy!

Incidentally, Netflix doesn't have a vacation or a dress-code policy. People still take holidays and no one comes to work naked (that actually is the only expectation the company has around clothing). The lesson they have learnt? *You don't need policies for everything.* Instead, there are "real values", specific behaviours, and skills they care about. One of these is inclusion. They believe that their deliberately diverse staff must know that they are accommodated and celebrated, not merely tolerated, for that difference.

They also value judgement, curiosity, communication, courage, selflessness and impact. It's worth taking a look at their explanation of the Netflix culture on their website.[12]

Netflix believes that if these real values are practised and visible in the way management and employees make decisions and work together with their partners and clients, there is no need for many of the policies

12 See https://jobs.netflix.com/culture/#introduction (accessed 14 February 2018)

that we spend time and energy creating. Or at least, the policies can be a lot shorter.

In the last few years, there has been a great deal of attention on policies in South African schools. The hair protests starting in Pretoria in 2016 forced schools to pull out (and journalists to download) uniform policies and codes of conduct. Incidents of racism in schools forced governing bodies to begin to include anti-racism policies in the list of documents that underpin how schools operate. And many schools are having to revisit their religious policies in the wake of the 2017 South Gauteng High Court ruling that schools may not favour one religion over others.

There is no doubt that school leaders for change need to relook at policies, codes of conduct, protocols, and processes within the school. In many cases, such as hair and uniform, what has been written in these policies, often many years ago, has had a detrimental impact on how young women (and men) see themselves in relation to others. Matthew Chaskalson, the attorney who argued for the Department of Basic Education in the 2017 South Gauteng High Court case, said, "Religious freedom is compromised when a policy divides the population into an inner circle that belongs, and an outer circle."[13] He could have also been referring to other freedoms that schools have compromised through their policies over the years.

These policies need to be looked at often, not just in times of crisis. How many schools revisit their uniform policy, or the code of conduct, on an annual basis? Surely, if these are the guiding documents of a school, they need to be looked at every year to see how they are responding to what is happening in or outside of the school. We need to be able

---

13 Greyling, J (17 May 2017), "Constitution Says Religion can be Practiced 'at', Not 'by' Schools, Court Hears", https://www.news24.com/SouthAfrica/News/constitution-says-religion-can-be-practiced-at-not-by-schools-court-hears-20170517 (accessed 8 March 2018).

to view these documents as we do the Constitution of the country – a document that was negotiated by people on different sides of the political, economic and social spectrum. Like the Constitution, we need to see our policies as living documents that are engaged and grappled with and amended when social, political and economic contexts change.

The process of relooking, rewriting and sometimes re-imagining is crucial. Policies need to be looked at with fresh eyes, almost as an outsider would looking in. Sometimes it might be useful to have people from outside the school, who are not necessarily from the dominant culture of the school or who don't have a vested interest in the school community, come in to help identify what needs to change. But it can also help to have the different, opposing, and sometimes quiet voices within the school look at the policies. They just need to be invited in. School policies, where they are still deemed necessary, need to become more transparent, negotiated, relevant and accessible documents.

As we have seen in Chapter 3, "Battling bias", people and institutions carry biases. It matters who is involved in policy writing and it matters how conscious they are of their biases (and the biases that the school as an institution has likely held over the years). There's a great deal of value in school leadership and staff being supported to continually move through a process of introspection, reflection, and consideration of their own biases (making time to take the Implicit Association Tests we referred to in Chapter 3, on page 80, for instance). Relooking at policies with these biases placed upfront can help to see the policies and procedures differently.

This reflection on school policies is part of the journey of awakening that teachers and leaders need to undergo themselves. It's about wanting to get this right. We need to train ourselves to see the world differently and embark on a journey that will allow each of us to view the world through the eyes of the other and so make the changes our schools need. In that process, we develop empathy, the ability to interact, and the ability to see the world from someone else's perspective. This is a liberating process that leads to the transformation of schools, people, and the communities they belong to.

This process also shifts the attention from the policies themselves to the behaviours and values of everyone in the school. Policies can be important and valuable for many schools. They can set a vision, they can set boundaries, and they can play a part in the nurturing and discipline needed in schools. But imagine if, like Netflix, a school adopted a more trusting, empowering and perhaps, liberating approach to some policies. Imagine a school's code of conduct reading:

> Act in the best interests of the school, those with whom you share this space, and yourself.

Just that.

For sure it's risky. For sure it would mean there would need to be a very conscious and deliberate plan to work on behaviours, values, and self-awareness in the school (for learners and adults). For sure the values, behaviours, and skills expected would need to be fleshed out, agreed upon, made visible, and role-modelled. But this approach could be tested with one policy for six months. If it doesn't work, the old policy returns. But if it works …

Well, then our attention is where it should be. Not on the words in documents we dust off in a crisis. Our attention would now be on the people, how they see themselves and the world, how they act and how they interact with each other.

It might be met with opposition. It might not work. But that's why we need leaders for change – visionary leaders who look ahead and take risks. We need visionary leaders who lead towards and through change.

And, of course, leaders who are happy with short sentences.

"You'd battle to find a school adopting any kind of transformative journey if the head of that school didn't believe in it. Conversely, if you've got a head who believes passionately in it, the journey is a much easier one to take. Because you influence. And you influence subtly – whether you're influencing through admissions policies, through language policies, you're influencing through the ceremonies that you have and how you conduct those ceremonies and if those are inclusive or exclusive.

One of the things I try and push quite hard with the school that I'm at is to make sure that what we do is relevant, and to make sure that what we do is relevant not only in South Africa but also in the world. Not only now but also in the future. So it's quite difficult – the marrying of a school that's over 100 years old and has had over 100 years' worth of tradition in a single-sex boys' environment which often comes across as being this very sort of traditionalist type space, and taking that space and saying, 'How can we best prepare our boys for a life out there that might be a little different?'

We have a code of conduct that is quite a lengthy document, but it's governed by these four values that we believe in, which is honour, integrity, respect, and then our fourth one is loyalty. Loyalty is not blind allegiance to something. It's just a loyalty to the organisation, people, friends, things like that. And then overarching all of this is this thing of, 'We cannot regulate for everything within our code of conduct, do good unto others and use your common sense.'"

Tony, **Principal**

"We're busy with looking at values at the moment because it came to thinking about the code of conduct and all the things that must be done through this transformation. But the discussion eventually got to the point where we said, 'Are the values that we stand by, and have stood by for the last 133 years, actually valid any more?' Because we must write every policy and every bit of our code of conduct according to our values. We started talking and now we're in the middle of a whole programme of looking at the values. Things like acceptance and diversity and inclusivity – these weren't values that we looked at 10 years ago, 15, 20 years ago. We're busy relooking and writing the values that are current for our current girls and that is quite an interesting process."

Shirley, **Principal**

6

FOSTERING CIVIL DISCOURSE

We have to create safe, controlled environments that allow young people to practise what it means to be a democratic citizen and to raise their views and opinions. We need to provide opportunities for them to learn to express their views while respecting those of others. They need to be taught to find consensus and how to understand the viewpoint of others, and that there's always an opportunity to engage with those who are different in order to find solutions that are better not in spite of, but because of our differences.

"Are schools preparing kids for the future? I don't think so. I think that South African schools which still follow quite a conservative model are preparing young people pretty much the same way they were ten years ago, and when I was at school in the 1990s. Those kinds of standard structures remain, of power ... Bringing civil discourse into classrooms is a starting point ... it could certainly spark a change within the culture of a given school."

Leah, **Teacher**

OWNING UP

In many staffrooms, some time well into the first term when the grade 8s have settled into high school, a conversation begins around cups of coffee and tea. You will hear something about the falling standards of the grade 8s coming through, how their grasp of arithmetic and language is just not up to standard. You might also hear something about who is to blame. The primary school teachers come up.

In another galaxy not too far away, in staffrooms on university campuses, another conversation is taking place about the calibre of the first-year students. Protests in which students have burnt down buildings and resorted to violence prompt another conversation about how unprepared these students are to be citizens. You will hear something about who is to blame for the students' inability to sit down, engage in civil discourse, and find solutions together. The high school teachers come up.

Perhaps teachers are to blame. Young people only begin to participate fully in democratic structures when they enter university. Yet, for the previous 12 years, they have been in authoritarian and controlled spaces. How do they deal with disagreements? They haven't developed the dialogue skills to help them engage with those who are older than them or even with their peers with whom they disagree. So they express their frustration with emotion, anger, and sometimes violence. We educators must take some responsibility for this. We have helped create this problem.

We have inherited an extremely authoritarian school system. During apartheid, the ruling party held a paternalistic view of the world. They knew best, and dictated what you needed to be thinking and what should be important to you. They believed theirs was the only legitimate view of the world, and silenced anyone who didn't agree. Schools mirrored this philosophy. The teachers, the principal, and the management of the school were the sources of all knowledge, truth and insight. Young people weren't given a voice or expected to have one.

Then we transitioned into a democracy. The very essence of a democracy is diverging viewpoints, the sense that an individual can hold their own beliefs, values and ideas and pursue these freely without any fear of intimidation or harm. But democracy hinges on the balance between these freedoms and the limits that arise from living in community with others. When our freedoms impinge on the freedoms and rights of others, it becomes a problem within society. Given that South Africa emerged from a time when the freedoms of the majority were restricted by the minority, it makes sense that this is not easily, nor immediately understood. It takes knowledge and practice to live in a democracy. More than 20 years later, we are still not fully equipped to be democratic citizens. We are still learning what this means.

It makes sense why living democratically, at times, feels a lot more like stumbling than striding.

Equally, we are still learning what it means to run schools in a democracy and to give a voice to young people. We can't ignore the fact that our schools, filled with young people born into a democracy, are run by adults who have come from an authoritarian background and have been part of a system that silenced voices. Most schools are still authoritarian environments, where young people are controlled, are told how they should dress, what hairstyles they are allowed, and how they must behave and speak. This is something we will continue to stumble over on our path into democratic living unless we deliberately decide to look down to see where we are placing our feet.

Much has been written about and in support of the South African school curriculum, which talks about schools as democratic spaces. But have the majority of schools really made the time and taken the risk to deliberately sit down together and ask how democracy happens in our schools? Given the increasing number of protests in schools and what young people are saying, it seems likely that we haven't sat down to listen to them. Yet we are living in a society where you are allowed to express your views and opinions, and are allowed to express these loudly and vociferously, even to people who might not want to hear what you have to say.

We need to allow young people to speak and be heard in our schools. That is work we, as adults, need to do on ourselves and our institutions. Equally, we need to prepare young people for a world in which they can speak out but also listen to and engage with views they don't agree with or understand.

We have to create safe, controlled environments that allow young people to practise what it means to be a democratic citizen and to raise their views and opinions. We need to provide opportunities for them to learn to express their views while respecting those of others. They need to be taught to find consensus and how to understand the viewpoint of others, and that there's always an opportunity to engage with those who are different in order to find solutions that are better not in spite of, but because of our differences.

In the introduction to *Fostering Civil Discourse – A Guide for Classroom Conversations*, which can be found in the Appendix on page 180, we argue why we need to very deliberately create the space to nurture and support democratic citizens and what it means to foster civil discourse in schools:

> In the midst of protests in South African schools over race and inclusion, ongoing protests on university campuses around fees and belonging, and a series of tragic acts of violence around the world, educators are rightly concerned about the lessons that today's learners might be absorbing about problem solving,

communication, civility, and their ability to make a difference. The next generation of South African voters needs models for constructive public discourse to learn from; the strength of our democracy requires it. But such examples seem few and far between.

How we talk about things matters, and we are not always well equipped. We may be able to share our views easily with those who already agree. But civil discourse is different, and it's critical to our ability to function as a democracy. How do we express our personal opinion while also leaving room for someone else's viewpoint? How do we engage when we may be embarrassed to reveal that we don't have all the information? How can we seek out or listen to those who hold different beliefs from our own and try to understand their point of view? How can we respectfully disagree?

We educators have an essential role to play. The classroom should be a place where learners learn to exchange ideas, listen respectfully to different points of view, try out ideas and positions, and give – and get – constructive feedback without fear or intimidation. Through engaging in difficult conversations, learners gain critical-thinking skills, empathy and tolerance, and a sense of civic responsibility.

There is no doubt we have work to do. There is no doubt we need to take some risks and need courage to engage in these difficult conversations in our classrooms and staffrooms. There is no doubt that it can be difficult and uncomfortable work to raise democratic citizens in our schools. But unless we begin to put this authentically at the centre of our school's vision and work very deliberately each day with each learner on this, those conversations in staffrooms on university campuses will become louder and louder, if only to be heard over the sounds of the violent clashes occurring outside their doors.

"We don't have any choice but to transform. If we don't, whatever is happening at the universities — we have seen a lot of these noises [about] transformation, curriculum and all those kinds of things — will go down to schools; believe me, it will go down. The best way is to start having this conversation, because if we don't, unfortunately, it's going to be imposed on us. There will be problems because then we will be caught maybe as if we were not even thinking about these things.

So that's why it is very important to look at your school, at the things that really need to be transformed, because if [we don't], unfortunately there will be challenges, transformation will now be imposed … believe me, from the learners themselves.

What's happening now at the tertiary level, we shouldn't think it's going to end there. These boys, I mean these kids, they are also looking. They are reading the news, they are watching these things, they see it going on and they feel, 'You know what, I think even at our school 1, 2, 3 is not okay. Let's stand up and address 1, 2, 3,' and we shouldn't wait for that. We shouldn't."

Meneer, **Principal**

"There was one lesson I did … because I was just tired of hearing very racist comments in my class. It was a lesson on prejudice. I wrote up a whole lot of words on the board and I said, 'Let's talk about stereotypes.' There was obviously that awkward beginning of, 'How do we deal with this? You can't write "gay" on the board, you can't write this on the board.' Then they started. And they started with stereotypes of Jewish people and then we got to black people and they couldn't stop talking, 'uncivilised …' I was sitting there taken aback. This is what, 2014, 2015.

I said white people next and there were two scholarship kids in our class from the local farming community. There was silence. Then one of them said, 'Spoilt', and the class erupted. I remember one girl in particular standing up and saying, 'Well, at least my father worked for my iPhone. Your parents choose not to work so you don't deserve one.' I mean from a teaching perspective I didn't know what to do, to be honest. I could see it was creating ripples in friendships and I felt like it was out of control. At the end of the class a grade 9 … the person who had said this about the iPhone … came right up to me – she was taller than me – and said, 'You will never talk about race or politics in your class again.'

I promptly emailed the parents … telling them that this had happened and encouraging them to continue the discussion at home.

But I think that grade, which would now be in matric, started talking more openly about these issues, whereas a lot of the parents at that particular school would certainly not have encouraged the kind of conversations we were having, these discussions about race and social justice. And with the change in management, those kinds of conversations became more prevalent."

Leah, **Teacher**

CIVIL DISCOURSE IN CLASSROOMS

The most exciting aspect of the transformation of schools is what is possible in the classroom. Within those four walls lies the possibility for a young person to experience, every day, what it is like to be acknowledged for who she is.

Within that classroom it is possible for her to feel a part of a community that operates upon the foundations of democracy, where everyone's opinion can be expressed, discussed and respected. The classroom is where she is heard, seen, and nurtured to thrive in a diverse and democratic society.

At its core, democracy is an acknowledgement that everyone has a contribution that should be allowed, valued, and respected. Instead of standing in front of the class and simply lecturing, teachers must encourage the learners to engage in that process of learning.

For a brief moment in our post-apartheid education journey, when we adopted Outcomes-Based Education (OBE), we spoke about the teacher as a facilitator. The learning process was meant to be one of self-discovery in which teachers would guide learners. Learners acquiring and discovering knowledge was as important as the knowledge itself. Given the inequality in the post-apartheid schooling system and the inability for it to withstand radical change, it is understandable why OBE failed. But along with it went the possibility for teachers to sometimes be facilitators and guiders of learning in the classroom. To support young people to flourish in a democracy, we need classroom environments that engage young people, where they can all put their ideas on the table to be debated and discussed by their peers, and the teacher. For that we need to allow back some part of the facilitator we lost when OBE was put to rest.

Co-author Roy has always entered the classroom with the aim of encouraging, guiding and challenging his learners to engage in civil discourse that prepares them to leave his watch better equipped as democratic citizens:

> Growing up in South Africa, I was the youngest in my family. Despite that, when it came to arguing, no special consideration was afforded me. There were 13 of us, and family conversation often ranged from politics to religion, from education to human rights. Debates were won based on the strength of our arguments and the passion with which we communicated them.
>
> It was in these moments that I first learned one of the most important lessons of discussion: respect for the person you are in conversation with. It was here that I learned to probe, prod, dissect, and dismantle the arguments of others. I realised the importance of respecting the views of others and the value in being open to re-evaluating my own preconceived ideas.
>
> Today, as an educator, why do I value debate, differing viewpoints, and the rights of others to think differently than I do? In large part it is because of these early experiences – both with my family and in school. My high school History teacher held a viewpoint on the political situation in South Africa in the early 1980s that was different from the views held by my church leaders. My siblings embraced a host of beliefs and convictions that were different from my parents'. (I suspect this was because it was impossible for my parents to

keep track of all 13 of us!) These dissenting voices helped me to develop the important skills of critical thinking and forced me to question myself and those around me. *Who do I believe? Why should I believe this point over that one? Why should I follow this ideology and not another?* It is this richness of opposing ideas that I wish to create in my classroom.

I try to foster this atmosphere in a number of ways. I approach teaching with an understanding that, as an educator, I am not a neutral conveyer of facts. I arrive at my classroom on any given day aware of my biases and value systems. Realising that I have my own predispositions and experiences allows me to "take them off", like a pair of spectacles. I can examine them and become aware of how they make me "see" the world. This makes me cautious and open to understanding that, even though I may have deeply held beliefs, they are simply choices I have made – they don't necessarily represent truth itself. My learners might hold a different truth from mine. The principal of my school might hold truths that are different from mine. The teacher in the classroom next door might hold different truths. This understanding helps me create a classroom that is rich with opportunities for debate and encouraging of challenges. I am aware of some of the baggage I bring into the classroom; it's the baggage I'm not aware of that's problematic. I need to confront my own prejudices and values, because it's only when I confront my reality that I can allow students to confront theirs.

> **"I try to foster this atmosphere in a number of ways. I approach teaching with an understanding that, as an educator, I am not a neutral conveyer of facts."**

I believe that young people are far more resilient than we often give them credit for. I show my learners that I will allow for my own views to be challenged, dissected, and even sometimes, discounted. This develops an environment of mutual respect where ideas, once voiced, become something we can all interact with, without it being attached to a particular ego or person.

Creating an environment that allows for democratic thinking and practices to emerge requires more than words. It requires that we, as teachers, live the values embodied in critical thinking. How can I expect learners to make themselves vulnerable and expose their ideas to criticism if I am not willing to do the same myself? How can I encourage my learners to become active citizens and challenge the people and practices that undermine democracy, and then fail to take any action myself in the face of injustice? Active citizenship that can transform communities and even countries requires first taking action in the immediate environment. Speaking up against "small" injustices often can be more impactful than looking for big causes to fight. Can we really tackle xenophobic violence when we turn a blind eye to bullying on the playground? Can we fight for a more accountable government if teachers at our own schools are not called to account? Teaching democratic values is not contained in a series of lessons; it is a lifestyle, an ethos that one creates in classrooms and the school as a whole.

To encourage active citizens who respect and value the democratic principles of our country's Constitution, it is important not only to pay attention to what happens in the classroom, but to also respect our learners' humanness in their lives beyond school and the four walls of the classroom. We must trust them to provide leadership. We must give them the time, space, and opportunity to grapple with these democratic values until they take root. We must spur them to action. And we must listen.

My job is to give my learners principles that will be of value to them throughout their lives. How do you live your life, in this world? How do you protect the basic principles of democracy, wherever you are? How do you ensure that you, as a democratic individual, live a life that's true to those beliefs and principles?

I don't know what my students will encounter when they leave my classroom and my direct influence on their lives. But I know that there are many other South Africans who are eager to rise above their pasts, and that they are increasing in number. And as long as people like that exist in the world, I hope that my students will encounter them and learn from their perspectives. I want them to be able to determine which views are worth having.

"In a city like Cape Town, the girls of colour that come from townships often have to go home, on long journeys … with difficulties. So girls perhaps play in the same sports teams but there's very little integration. The integration at the moment predominantly happens in the classroom. So I think that is where staff, teaching staff, should actually be saying, 'What opportunities can I create for conversations to happen so that we get to know each other better?' You set up your rules, you say in this space [that] this is how we behave, that we foster respect. You create the space to talk, and I think out of that dialogue comes a lot of understanding of the other. When you learn to listen to another person and actually get to know that person more intimately, you have a different perspective than when you just made assumptions, or had preconceived ideas that have come out of your own prejudices.

I feel that creating a space in every classroom, whether you are teaching Maths, or whether you're teaching Science, or whether you are teaching subjects that more easily lend themselves to talking about democracy, it has to be done. It does not matter what field you study, what expertise you learn, what occupation you do one day, you remain a human being who will work with other human beings. You will need to do group activities, you will need to treat people every day as you wish to be treated, you will work with issues of poverty, of wealth, of gender discrimination. And I just think it gives the pupils in your class the tools to actually become a leader in that field, or to even know, on a human level, how to actually make somebody feel included.

For me it goes way beyond the academic and intellectual. It's not just looking at the mind and getting knowledge and listening to feedback from people, it's also about your heart. What I've also discovered with girls that I teach [is that] they often become disillusioned because the problems seem so big, and so large, and they never know where to begin and how they could possibly change this. My deliberate message to them is, 'Start small. You start one to one. You are dealing with people in shops every day, you're dealing with people at the traffic lights every day, you are greeting staff at school, you are working with your friends, or girls that you're not necessarily friendly with. Your words have to be consciously adjusted to include people, and to be reflective about yourself.'

For me, education is a multi-faceted concept. It is about drawing out the capacity of every human being to make them a better human being, and that's why I feel teachers have this awesome responsibility. We're not perfect. I don't think we even manage to do a small portion of that. But if you see every child that you have in your classroom as having potential as a human being … the way that you treat that child will have an impact on them for the rest of their lives. So it's also creating the discourse, perhaps in a dysfunctional society where things are not equal."

Sue, *Teacher*

7

WHERE
TO BEGIN

Schools need practical places to start (and sometimes, to continue) the journey of transformation. In this chapter, you will find ideas for taking the next step in transforming your school in the six areas of transformation identified and addressed in the previous chapters of this book. The ideas are wide-ranging, and deliberately so — from simple to complex, from those requiring financial resources to those that don't, and from suggestions that take a few days to implement to those that will take much longer. There is something here for every school, no matter where you are on your journey or your access to resources.

For more information about workshops and implementation support we offer schools, please visit www.aschoolwhereibelong.com

"I think it's true that I've benefitted a lot from the school that I went to and the education I received there, but I don't think we should feel that the sense of feeling beholden to the school should somehow preclude me from criticising the aspects of the institution that I think are problematic. I think it's wholly possible for the school to carry on producing academically excellent students whilst undoing many of the more harmful and problematic features of the school. I don't think the two are somehow mutually exclusive. I think in fact the two reinforce each other — I think producing excellent students and being a racist institution often are incompatible. I think the more you disabuse yourself of those biases the better students you'll produce."

Markus, **Former Learner**

FACING THE PAST

Develop a shared 20-year vision for the school and the community it is a part of.

- This vision-building exercise should include all stakeholders (parents, educators, learners, and community members). Preferably, the robust voices of young people must be given prominence in this process. After all, the exercise entails imagining a school, community, and country that they (and their children) will live in. Some initial focus questions might be:
  - In 20 years' time, what do we want the school to be like, look like and feel like for the learners and staff who will be here?
  - Who do we think will be attending our school?
  - What will inclusion and transformation look like?
  - What do we currently have in place that can set us on this journey?
  - What do we need to do differently?
  - What do we need to begin?

- This vision of the future must be discussed, debated and shared within the wider school community, because, in a very real sense, it is only when there is agreement on a common future that we can usefully revisit the past to ask ourselves two critical questions:
  - What in the past is preventing us from achieving that future we imagine?
  - What in our past can contribute to creating that future we desire?

Arrange a two-day *Facing the Past*[14] workshop or similar programme.

- Give teachers the time and facilitated safe space to understand:

---

14 Visit www.shikaya.org for more information.

- our apartheid history (bearing in mind that fewer than 15% of all South Africans study History beyond grade 9, 85% of South Africans have a very superficial understanding of our past!).
- how each of our identities were shaped in that time.
- the choices that all South Africans made during apartheid.
- the categories that people occupy during times of gross human-rights violations – victims, perpetrators, bystanders, upstanders, and resistors.
- the call to change or action that this knowledge of the past creates for us individually and collectively.

Look at how we write our history.
- With a diverse team representing the variety of voices in the school, critically look at how the history of your school is presented on your website and in your school archives or marketing material.
    - Does it, for example, acknowledge when the school became open to all races? Does it highlight this as one of the most important events in the history of the school? What message would it send out if this moment was given prominence?
    - Who (individuals and groups) is given prominence and status? Does this exclude groups at your school?
    - How could you include a recognition that some people were not allowed to attend your school? (Perhaps even a recognition that the school might have been complicit in that.) What message would this send out?

"We happened to be in the middle of a big building project, and one of the names was particularly colonial, which was the [name of the] quad. This particular quad was about to be built, and a new space was going to be created. We had a name-changing committee working, and in discussion they decided that this was probably a great space because it had changed.

Each grade had a meeting and had to suggest as many names as they wanted. Once again, nothing was compulsory. If you wanted to come to the discussion, there was a time during the school day when each grade could meet. They all had to put together their names, but each name had to be motivated. From those names they had to choose the top three. Each grade did this and the staff did exactly the same thing. So eventually we landed up with these 18 top names from five grades and the staff.

They then were put on a list and we all had to vote for our top one … The top-five list was duly presented to the School Governing Body who turned around and said, 'It's not our space, it belongs to you.' We eventually decided that they would remove any name that they felt had any ambiguities, that they felt they weren't comfortable with. So out of the top five they removed three eventually and left two. They then gave it back to the RCL [Representative Council of Learners] and said, 'You now must go back to the girls.'

So we decided on a democratic vote for the last part. They came into the hall and they voted at booths so that nobody could discuss what it was that they were voting for. It actually eventually did not go with one of the African languages, which everybody had imagined it would. It actually took one of the words of our motto and the quad was named for that. So all the fear about changing, for me, for the past pupils, all fell away because the motto has been from when we started 133 years ago. And the fact that the current girls actually subscribed to having that as the new quad name brought in the past pupils – they felt that was okay.

I just believe that the way it's been done will make future name changes so much easier because the first one has been successful. It's been accepted. It absolutely has made little difference on the ground, but everybody felt that they were part of it, and everybody felt that they had a say."

Shirley, **Principal**

DELIBERATELY INCLUDING

Conduct a thorough review of every aspect of school life – from sports to cultural activities; from academic awards to clubs and societies. Bring a representative group of learners, parents, and teachers together from across the various groups for this review.

Some key questions to focus on could be:

- Does this sport/award/club/activity exclude any group within the school?
- If yes, is this exclusion deliberate, and is it justifiable? (e.g. Academic awards are by their nature exclusionary, but they can be justified by saying that they create healthy competition and a desire to do better. That said, awards might be made more inclusive, for example by recognising improvements in results or perseverance, or awarding more broadly outside of academic and sporting excellence.)
- The same question has to be asked of exclusions that were not deliberate: Is it justified?
- Small things matter. Look at who gets to speak in assemblies and who is invited as guest speakers throughout the year and at prize-giving. Do these speakers represent the dominant culture of the school? Who can you invite who represents minority groups, or the minority culture, in your school?
- Do the photos and images displayed around the school only represent the history of the school that might have excluded others?
- What religion dominates in assemblies? How could this be excluding others? Even if yours is a private school that is set up with an emphasis on a particular religion, how can other faiths be included in moments when the school gathers? If yours is a public school, should any religion

be allowed a particular dominance? Could the school still teach values and behaviours without emphasising any one religion? Engage parents, learners and alumni who do not represent the dominant religion of the school, and begin a conversation around how they feel about their religion not being given space or valued. Ask what the school could do to rectify this. It may not be possible to address all needs, but addressing some concerns can go a long way in building trust and showing that all learners are valued.

Review the code of conduct.
- No one should be excluded by what has been written down in the code of conduct. While some codes of conduct have deliberately (or unconsciously) excluded some learners at schools, the code of conduct has the ability to include and unite people.
- The code of conduct should value and respect difference within the community rather than simply trying to integrate everyone into the dominant/historical culture. This is an opportunity to create a new sense of community.
- Expand this review beyond educators and school management to include parents and the Representative Council of Learners, who will fulfil their legal mandate and be the voice of their peers. Include representatives who are not from the dominant culture.

Begin the conversation.
- So many people we have spoken to have emphasised the need for conversations – especially with those who disagree, who have different views and who are not from the dominant culture of the school.
- While it is natural to fear these conversations because they deal with sensitive issues, avoiding the conversations is something greater to fear. Some school leaders have said that they fear having these conversations in case they get out of control. Our answer has always

been that it is when the conversations don't take place that things spiral. It doesn't mean that the conversations won't be hard and emotional or that things won't get heated and we will all agree. But if the conversations are started with the intention of listening and hearing why groups are feeling as they do, then the outcome can be one of healing and growth. Since schools became multi-racial in the 1990s, very few real conversations have taken in place. Within an overwhelming climate of assimilation, hearing each other has not been a priority or seen as a need.

- These conversations can happen in different ways. Some might want outside consultants to facilitate them to ensure they remain orderly. Also, some may feel that the school community would respond better to a neutral party, and more honest discussions can take place. Bringing outsiders in might be a very good way to begin. But at some point, schools need to engage in these discussions by themselves. (See principal Murray's description of the dialogue on discrimination on pages 107-09 for a powerful example of what is possible in schools.)

- Key in these discussions is that everyone is included and the teachers and leadership approach these dialogues with the intention of listening and learning, not responding and solving.

"We've seen in the last couple of years that schools need to change and have a very serious look at who they are. They need to change the attitude of saying, 'You fit into what we are,' as opposed to saying, 'This is our school.'

So the use of all these words, 'us' and 'them' and 'we', is so important in the language of transformation and the language of diversity … but a lot of people have said, 'You knew what the school was like before you came here. Why didn't you just fit into what the rules are?' I think that's archaic, I think that that kind of approach is arrogant, it's superior, it's saying that, 'I'm better than you so you've got to come and fit into my ways.' It says, 'I don't have to see you, I don't have to acknowledge you,' and I think that that's wrong.

I speak to boys often about dialogue and I say to them that dialogue is a critical part of us growing as a school, as a nation. Whatever we're doing, we've got to remember to listen to each other, because we're all very keen to talk but we're not that keen to listen. So let's just listen and say, 'So you've come into the school that I happen to be in and I happen to work in. I'd like to hear your story, I'd like to hear — what do you think about this?' You know, one of the first questions I asked children is I'd say to them, 'What's it like to be black at the school that I'm at, which is a predominantly white school?'"

Tony, *Principal*

"I think a person's got to be very deliberate about inclusion because I do feel that you have to explicitly show an attitude of acceptance. You've got to create the opportunity to say, 'I want to hear what contribution you can make,' or, 'I want to hear what makes you unhappy,' or, 'I want to hear from you how you felt when this happened,' or, 'How would you feel if this rule was changed?' You're not only role-modelling an attitude that is more open-minded, you are also creating the opportunity for that dialogue to happen. And I do think, explicitly in our classrooms, we can expedite that through methodology. It's the book that you choose to read as a reader, it's the holiday read that you give girls to read on their own and then come back to a discussion. It's the history of a community, or an individual, who children who feel ostracised can now identify with, so it's saying your history is as important as what we determine our history to be."

Sue, *Teacher*

BATTLING BIAS

Begin with you.

- While transforming schools and creating inclusive environments involves rethinking policies, is about numbers and quotas, and requires hard work, the most important work is working on ourselves. The policies won't really change until we do.
- Until we can listen to ourselves, we can't really listen to others. We have to be willing to set aside the time, expect that it will be difficult, and remain open to being honest with others, but most importantly, ourselves.
- If we don't see transformation as something that begins with each one of us, we will never really find ourselves working and thriving in transformed schools.

Make time for reflection.

- Great teachers are reflective teachers who are on a continual journey of self-awareness.
- Management needs to set aside time for teachers to reflect – on their identities, how they see each other, and how they feel about what is happening in society or in their schools.
- Teachers need time to share in their reflection with colleagues. This helps us see ourselves and each other differently. It builds relationships and teams.
- Allocate time in the Professional Development plan for reflection. Set aside 20 minutes every Friday for teachers to reflect in journals (see page 158), and to share some of their thoughts with colleagues. If possible start school 20 minutes later on a Friday, or gather staff 20 minutes before school begins on Fridays (that's their commitment to the process), and this reflection session doesn't interrupt the teaching day.

Buy journals.

- Give teachers journals to support the practice of reflection and awareness. Buy journals that are visually striking to emphasise that the exercise of journaling is valued.

- Journaling is a very useful tool to focus attention and thinking and, especially in busy schools, to force some time for quiet and centring.

- Once a week, for 20 minutes at the start of the day (see above), every teacher sits in the staffroom and writes in their journal. They then pair up with a colleague and share a few of the thoughts they are comfortable sharing.

- Of course, there will be resistance, but journaling and reflection is a practice and a discipline. Facilitate the practice so that there is a shared focus. For example, for a month, ask teachers to reflect on how they are seeing inclusion and exclusion playing out in their classrooms. What are they noticing? What can they do more of? What can they do less of?

- Try it for a month, with four sessions, to ease into it. If it doesn't work, end the experiment. But remember, even if just a few teachers find value and adopt it, that's a start. The focus then is to allow them to continue and later share with the rest of the staff how it has shifted things inside of them and their classroom. Don't forget the early adopters!

- Imagine, though, if it does work. Imagine the environment in the staffroom when teachers are regularly reflecting, sharing, and opening up. Imagine what that can do for the classroom environment.

- It doesn't have to end with the teachers. The entire school could spend 20 minutes once a week, or even just twice a term, reflecting on and sharing how they are seeing themselves and others, what is changing, and what is staying the same. See page 187 of the Appendix for ways of using journals in classrooms.

Take the Implicit Association Test.

- Set aside an hour from the Professional Development plan for the staff to take the Implicit Association Test (see https://implicit.harvard.edu/implicit/).

- The test is not perfect, and the results do not define the person. They simply suggest that you might have a natural, unconscious bias for or against different groups of people. So do the test a few times!

- Invite staff to own the test results – not to justify, dismiss, or explain them away! Ask them to journal how they feel about the result. Were they surprised? Why? How do they feel? Why? Could this bias be impacting on their relationships and their teaching?

- In the remaining time, teachers pair up and share what they feel comfortable sharing, again with an emphasis on the results not defining the person. Provide some indication of behaviours we might want to address. Ask staff to offer each other advice.

- In another Professional Development session, return to the test results. Give teachers time to reflect and share anything they have discovered since taking the test.

Make a plan.

- Based on the process above, staff members should develop their own personal action plan to address their implicit biases as they play out with colleagues and learners. They should share this action plan with an accountability partner – someone, possibly not their best friend – who can gently check them on their progress.

- Accountability partners should, in a non-judgemental way, notice behaviours or interactions their partners might not be aware of, and point out when implicit biases might be manifesting in micro or overt aggressions.

- Suggest the following things staff can do to address their unconscious biases.

Become more aware

After taking the IAT, reflect on interactions you have had and will continue to have with people you have a bias for or against. How did you behave? Was it different to interactions with other people? How did you feel? Simply creating the space to be more aware allows your conscious brain to take over more control.

Individuate

Accept that you are not colour-blind. You do see colour and difference. When you are with people you hold a negative bias against, make an effort to remember individual characteristics – their names, mannerisms, and interests. The more you do this, the more you force the brain to not see them as simply an Out Group.

Expose yourself to counter-stereotypes

If you have a bias that sees women as less capable in the workplace, expose yourself to women who counter this. Read more books by women authors or invite women in leadership positions to talk at your school. The more you deliberately counter the stereotypes that your unconscious brain understands, the more you take control back.

(For school leaders: What is the dominant culture in your school? Given that, what are the unconscious biases that the majority of people at the school likely hold? How do you counter that by creating opportunities for the learners and teachers to hear from, be taught by, and be inspired by those they likely have a negative bias towards?)

Engage in positive interactions with members of groups you hold a bias against

The interactions need to be positive because your brain is hardwired to remember more negative aspects of people in your Out Group. But positive interactions do not need to just be fun. Learning together can be a positive interaction. Working together to achieve a common goal can be a positive interaction.

Mere contact between group members isn't enough. Meaningful, ongoing relations are important. This takes effort and planning. What interactions do you need to plan for your learners (and staff) to have over the course of the year or multiple years that allow for meaningful and ongoing relations to emerge with people you likely hold a negative bias towards?

Take it to the classroom

Introduce and discuss implicit bias in the classroom. Ask learners to reflect on their own implicit bias (possibly let them do the IAT). How do they see bias playing out in the school and in your classroom? Develop a class strategy to deal with implicit bias in a way that makes everyone aware of it, that is non-judgmental, is supportive, and encourages positive change.

Take it into the office.

All management members interviewing staff for new or promotion positions should discuss their IAT results with other committee members. This should be an open process and the team should work out ways to minimise the possibility of implicit bias influencing hiring decisions. Put questions and processes in place to mitigate implicit bias. If all members of the interview panel share the same implicit bias it could be an indication that the panel needs to be more diverse.

"I think personal bias is one of the biggest stumbling blocks to achieving trustful and trustworthy relationships between the pupil body and the teacher body. My experience in the context of where I teach is that the majority of teachers tend to defensively say, 'I'm not racist, I'm not biased, I've done nothing wrong.' They come from that position of almost entitlement, where they say, 'I'm the teacher. I'm the authority figure. I don't need to change because I've done nothing wrong.'

I took the Implicit Association Test and it did reveal interesting things to me. Some I could have predicted, perhaps. But it's made me realise again that all of us have biases and prejudices that we need to deal with. The reason why people [don't] take the Implicit Association Test is because they don't want to know. They just think, 'Ja, it's a test, what do they know about me?' I think it's a bit of denial: 'I'm not going to do it because then I don't need to confront it.'

Trust is one of the building blocks of a society where you want inclusion. So the girls need to feel that there's an open-mindedness where it's a safe space to talk about these things because the adults in that space are allowing it, and also guiding it. They are also saying, 'We've made errors.' Teachers need to say, 'We've made errors. We are authority figures. We need to reflect and look at our own prejudices.' There's a kind of recognition that the growth will only come if we all actually take a step forward, and in that way you'll get the kind of dialogue that you're looking for.

These kinds of platforms need to be created, and the girls will only come forward and talk if you have that kind of inclusive approach where you're saying, 'We acknowledge that we need to improve our understanding and our empathy for where you are at, and therefore let's try and get dialogue going that will be beneficial to all.' That kind of opening up and open-mindedness creates the opportunity for dialogue. If you don't do that and you smugly sit and say, 'We've done nothing wrong,' you're going to struggle to get any kind of inclusivity in that kind of environment."

Sue, **Teacher**

SEEKING DIFFERENCE

Start in the staffroom.
- Create opportunities for groups to interact who do not traditionally do so.
  Some simple suggestions:
    - At internal staff-development sessions, be deliberate about seating arrangements so that staff move out of their comfort zones and affirming groups.
    - Identify a few "agitators" who will deliberately break boundaries and sit with groups they do not normally sit with.
    - Instead of a social for the whole staff every term, have smaller social opportunities. Arrange (and pay for) the Maths and Drama departments to go for coffee and cake. Mix it up!
    - Whole-staff development programmes should have a team-building component to them that deliberately groups people who do not normally interact with one another.

In the classroom.
- Through subtle measures, such as being deliberate about seating arrangements and group-work pairings, get your learners to explore new interactions and relationships.

On the playground.
- If groups form based almost exclusively on ethnicity, be brave and begin a discussion about this with your Representative Council of Learners and prefects. Focus assembly talks around the courage we all need to move from where we feel comfortable with our In Group to where it's uncomfortable stepping towards our Out Group.
- Move beyond merely asking learners to explain why they prefer to

interact only with those in their In Group, remind them of the common future you agreed to build (which forms part of your strategic plan that was developed in consultation with all the stakeholders of the school community), and ask them to join you in finding ways to use the playground to bring people of different groups together without prescribing friendships.

Acknowledge the voice and role of the Representative Council of Learners.
- Endorse and speak about the RCL's roles and responsibilities of representing all the learners.
- Ensure RCL members are adequately trained to fulfil their responsibilities.
- Ensure the RCL's voice is heard at management and School Governing Body level.
- Ensure that there are clear channels through which the RCL can raise matters and receive feedback, showing that the school management wishes to operate in an environment of mutual accountability and to hear different voices.
- The RCL must be encouraged to continuously create opportunities for learners to express their concerns, make suggestions and bring about change at the school. The more they can do this, the more the voices of a wide range of learners can be heard.

Partner with a school that's different.
- Seek and develop a partnership with a school that is very different to yours. It could be a school from a historically disadvantaged area. The intention is to build a partnership that is mutually reinforcing, in which staff and learners from each school get to authentically engage and learn from and with each other. This is not a charity initiative. This is about the schools developing and learning together.

Establish an international student-exchange programme.

- Many schools across the world are looking to partner with South African schools in exchange programmes.
- Use technology to link learners from different cultures, communities and countries.
- The programme's focus should be on understanding difference and the value it can bring into learners' personal, school and community environments.

Teach for difference.

- Establish, through the curriculum and extra-curricular activities, regular opportunities to learn about different cultures (both far and near). This can be through the books teachers choose to introduce to the learners and the speakers invited in.
- The aim is to create a comfortableness around difference, rather than a mere tolerance for it.

Focus on feeder schools.

- High schools need to monitor their feeder schools to make sure they are deliberately seeking out difference in their admissions policy.
- Place a moratorium on accepting learners from schools performing poorly in this regard. Nothing forces change as swiftly as real consequences in the real world – remember, part of that primary school's marketing strategy is that their learners are accepted at your high school!
- Improve your school's ability to identify learners who meet criteria in order to start, with confidence, recruiting from primary schools and communities that you have not traditionally accessed.

Recruit differently.

- Principals of former Model-C schools and private schools are often only able to identify suitable candidates for staff positions when the applicants have experience at former Model-C or private schools. Principals must develop the skills and processes to be able to reliably identify good staff from schools that are outside of their immediate purview. This means initiating and building relationships with the leadership of these schools. The Department of Education provides opportunities for principals to do this with the plethora of meetings that are called on a regular basis.

- Develop a protocol of how interview committees are constructed. An overarching question should be, "Does this committee have enough difference and diversity in order to give every candidate a fair chance at succeeding?"

Transform the admissions policy.

- Where a school is in an affluent area and draws most of its learners from the surrounding neighbourhoods, the leadership needs to re-look the admissions policy. A deliberate attempt needs to be made to make it possible for learners from outside the area and from different income levels to attend the school.
- This may involve restructuring fees or creating a model that allows for differentiated fee contribution according to family income (beyond the current government-exemption criteria).
- The admissions policy should be transparent and it should not be left up to one or two individuals in management to decide who gets into the school.
- Conduct an audit of the learners being admitted, focusing on race and where they live. Without this information, it is difficult to set targets and put plans in place to change the demographics.
- Ensure that the admissions policy, currently and in future, aligns with the Constitution and the South African Schools Act, especially in light of recent court rulings that limit the ability of schools to exclude learners for various reasons.

"We've also got an intern programme … where if there is a young black person who hasn't finished his or her qualification yet, who has to pay [for] the qualification … for them to teach a limited number of classes [at our school] while under a mentorship or under a mentor's guidance. But it's tough. It's tough to find, to try to make our staff a little bit more representative of our student population.

I don't know how one necessarily actively goes to find and actively recruits teachers. I've never done that. It's kind of strange. I know some teachers of the past, and I'm not talking about race — we're talking about getting young men into the teaching profession, who would go into universities and … try to speak to the young men who were studying to become teachers. And perhaps that is the way to go, that one needs to go into an environment and say, 'I'm looking.' And to be honest with people and say, 'Look, I'm looking particularly for young black teachers … I think my staff is not properly representative of the student population or of South Africa, so I'm looking for young black teachers, please help me.'"

Tony, **Principal**

LEADING FOR CHANGE

Admit a lack of preparation.
- Principals must accept that the very experience at similar schools that got them their jobs could be a liability rather than an asset when it comes to leading a school to transform.
- School leaders need to deliberately expose themselves to environments, speakers, books and people who can challenge and extend their thinking rather than merely endorsing it. It will involve seeking out that which is uncomfortable and different.

Develop a new formula for the school's success.
- The formula used to ensure the past success of the school will not ensure its success going forward.
- Past success becomes the enemy of continued excellence because it no longer takes into account a changed society in which success has been redefined.
- School leaders must use the outcome of the vision-building exercise on page 147, to start formulating a clear strategy to achieve transformation.

Retreat to reflect.
- Organise a leadership retreat where the main focus is reflecting on:
  - personal leadership values and character.
  - leaving a personal and professional legacy.
  - the degree to which personal choices and values act as inhibitors or contributors to constructive change at the school.

Construct a diverse leadership team.
- Great schools are run by a team. South African schools going forward need to have diverse leadership teams.

- Deliberately construct a leadership team that reflects diversity. This is the only appropriate check and balance that ensures that change is thoughtful and considerate of all.
- Identify who you need on your team to ensure diversity of perspective and put together a commitment and a plan for this. Recruit for this. Head-hunt for this. Be deliberate.
- If there are no positions open or likely to be open soon, seriously consider expanding the team. Schools have the ability to create the leadership team as they see fit. New positions can be created, SMT (Senior Management Team) positions can be rotated every two or three years, and management structures can be flattened out to provide more leadership opportunities to others. Remuneration might be an issue. Given the finances that many schools have access to, however, money should not be a stumbling block. It might just mean that some capital projects could be put on hold or a different fundraising pitch needs to be made.

Revisit policies annually.
- Every year, policies should be revisited from a diverse range of perspectives, including those of parents, teachers, learners and alumni.
- Bring the Representative Council of Learners into the process. Allow the RCL to comment on policies (after all, the South African Schools Act allows them to), to say whether they work for them, and if they are policies that develop the learners. The RCL's comments don't have to be automatically accepted, but their voice (like those of the parents and educators) needs to be heard and engaged with.
- Invite alumni into this conversation, especially those who represent diverse groups or voices. Alumni often still love their school deeply. Understand that dissenting voices, or voices that are difficult to hear, aren't meant to be destructive. They are meant to be helpful and to assist the school to navigate the difficult process of transition. Instead of waiting for alumni to comment negatively on social media about

policies and experiences, and for it to spiral out of control, invite and embrace their comments. Create spaces where they can speak about their experiences. Make use of reunions as opportunities not just to look back but to look forward together, to gather information that would be useful for the school and the school's path forward.

- Management should commit to taking recommendations seriously. Very few policies should be set in stone (barring those, like policies on safety and drugs, that a school legally needs to commit to and uphold), but aspects of the code of conduct and the religious policy, for example, can be revisited, given changing times, contexts and learners and staff.
- Not everything has to change every year. Consistency and stability are needed, but in opening up the discussion and possibility, some rational and authentic middle ground can be found.

Live the values.
- All schools highlight certain values that are meant to underpin the policies that govern the school.
  - How visible are these in everyday interactions?
  - How can these be deliberately lived by staff and learners?
  - Are there new values that need to be included? Just like traditions, the values that were needed in the past might not be the values needed now. Given that the school is on a path of transforming the demographics of learners and staff, the school's values need to be reflective of everyone. They might be already, but that can only be known if these questions are asked.
- Following a similar process to revisiting policies, revisit the values of the school with a diverse and broad group of stakeholders. This needn't be an annual undertaking. Every five years, create the opportunity for all learners to engage with the values, reflect on them, and offer their opinions or suggestions. The more learners are brought into the conversation, the more the values become real to them.

Audit traditions, practices and names.

- Assemble a traditions-audit team made up of a group of staff, alumni, parents and learners. This team needs to be diverse and include a variety of voices. It is crucial that during the audit process the team ensures that all voices are heard and valued.
- Have the audit team invite all alumni, staff and learners to submit a list of traditions, practices and names they feel should remain, change or be created. These could include grade 8 orientation practices, the names of houses, awards and buildings. It is important that, along with the submissions, participants explain why they feel the way they do. The team will use this as the basis for the audit.
- Using the submissions, create a list that, for each tradition, practice and name, answers the following questions:
  - What is the purpose of the tradition?
  - Who/what does it represent?
  - Why is it important today that this continues?
  - Why should it be changed?
  - Who can identify with the tradition, practice or name? Who cannot?
  - Who is being excluded by this?
  - What could we lose by changing this?
  - What could we change?
  - Could something new be added?
- Collate this information into a document and present it back to the school community for comment.

Take on a tradition.

- Once the audit of traditions is complete and the school community have given their input, choose the three traditions, names or practices that the school community feel most strongly about, or the ones that most clearly exclude some learners at the school. Focus on one of these as the starting point.

- Take on that tradition. The example quote from principal Shirley, on page 175, shows the value of taking on one tradition at a time and the importance of understanding why learners and alumni feel the way they do. The approach Shirley and her school took of engaging everyone in the school community and giving voice to the learners is a useful model to learn from.

"You know, sometimes it's difficult to put your finger on what makes a person shift, but for me, I think it was just listening and listening and listening, and hearing more and more why people felt how they did. And so often, I think, in our world we hear that people want to do something but we don't stop to listen as to why they want to do it. So the more I heard why, and the hurt that people felt, the more I realised that I could … be more in their shoes and look at it from a different angle. And so the shift for me became, 'So what is a name? Is it actually the essential part of the school?' And no, it isn't.

There are girls that have never had the chance to be part some of the old traditional schools with the resources they've had, and I do think we need to acknowledge that. An interesting thing happened just this week. We were talking about Founders' Day and how we could acknowledge not only the founding of our school, which is the traditional model, but to in some way acknowledge that there were many people who couldn't attend our school, and there were many people who struggled, who went through the struggle, who were activists, to get to the point of allowing the girls who are currently there.

.

So I think it is important and we're looking for ways. One is in our new rituals, or ceremonies – [to show] that we are cognisant of the fact, that we acknowledge our past in some way. We haven't come to the perfect sort of process yet, and we're working on it. We had a discussion this week and we'll come back again and again. But just to find a way in which we can acknowledge that there are people who would have died to come to our schools, and some of them did die so that their kids can get here, and their children want to say something, their children want to acknowledge that past."

Shirley, **Principal**

FOSTERING CIVIL DISCOURSE

Foster discourse in the classroom.
- Plan to include at least one of the methodologies explained in the *Fostering Civil Discourse* manual (in the Appendix) per month. These are designed to facilitate dialogue, discussion and reflection. Evaluate the methodology's effectiveness by including your own observations and those of your learners. Share your experience with other staff.
- Ensure all educators are trained in the use of teaching methodologies that create safe and inclusive environments for all.
- Use these methodologies in staff meetings, especially when it is important that all viewpoints are heard on a matter. This inculcates certain behaviours and good practices in the school.

Work with the Representative Council of Learners.
- Using some of the methodologies from the *Fostering Civil Discourse* manual in the Appendix, run workshops with your RCL on complex issues facing society and the school. Ensure that the RCL understands both its legal role as representatives of the learners as well as the critical social role it plays in ensuring that a cohesive community is structured within the school that serves all stakeholders well.

Create opportunities for engagement and dialogue.
- Create forums that engender discussion and healthy debate. This could be through existing societies and clubs or through creating new ones. Invite learners from other schools and communities to ensure that the debates allow for different world views and perspectives.

Bring in different viewpoints.

- Use moments when the entire school body is together to expose learners to a wide variety of perspectives on matters affecting society or the school community.

"I think it need not be so clear in the sense that, 'Today we are going to talk about race in South Africa.' I think you start with general issues, I think you start with things that aren't loaded and aren't, actually to be honest, local.

So I would start with something far away. You start with something quite straightforward in a discussion where everyone in that classroom can have an opinion. And it's distant opinion. Because if you start with something local, if you start with something charged, it's already going to be, 'Well, that person said that because ...'

Especially with teenagers, especially at these kinds of privileged schools, they tend to have a sense of confidence and they tend to have opinions on the death penalty or whatever it is. I think you start slowly like that.

When people feel that they have their opinion on whatever issue it is, however distanced or detached they are from it, then you can start saying, 'Okay, well, let's look at these things at home. Let's look at where our responsibility lies. Do we even have any responsibility?'

You can play devil's advocate. I think that's also important in schools where everyone's politically correct. Playing devil's advocate so that you don't always have, 'I agree, I agree, I agree, I agree, I agree,' because that's what you should do. You can't get anywhere with everyone agreeing. You can't actually have any meaningful debate."

Leah, **Teacher**

APPENDIX

FOSTERING CIVIL DISCOURSE – A GUIDE FOR CLASSROOM CONVERSATIONS

This guide was produced for South African educators by Facing History and Ourselves. To download the guide as a free PDF and to learn more about the work of Facing History and Ourselves with Shikaya in South Africa, please visit www.facinghistory.org and www.shikaya.org

Civil discourse in South Africa is critical to our ability to function as a democracy. This resource provides some tools to help prepare classrooms and learners to practise civil discourse, an essential skill for effective civic participation.

*

In the midst of protests in South African schools over race and inclusion, ongoing protests on university campuses around fees and belonging, and a series of tragic acts of violence around the world, educators are rightly concerned about the lessons that today's learners might be absorbing about problem solving, communication, civility, and their ability to make a difference. The next generation of South African voters needs models for constructive public discourse to learn from; the strength of our democracy requires it. But such examples seem few and far between.

How we talk about things matters, and we are not always well equipped. We may be able to share our views easily with those who already agree. But civil discourse is different, and it's critical to our ability to function as a democracy. How do we express our personal opinion while also leaving room for someone else's viewpoint? How do we engage when we may be embarrassed to reveal that we don't have all the information? How can we seek out or listen to those who hold different beliefs from our own and try to understand their point of view? How can we respectfully disagree?

We educators have an essential role to play. The classroom should be a place where learners learn to exchange ideas, listen respectfully to different points of view, try out ideas and positions, and give – and get – constructive feedback without fear or intimidation. Through engaging in difficult conversations, learners gain critical-thinking skills, empathy and tolerance, and a sense of civic responsibility.

On the following pages, we have provided some tools to help prepare your classroom and your learners to practise civil discourse, an essential skill for effective civic participation, including:

- Developing a reflective classroom community
- Creating a classroom contract
- Providing opportunities for learner reflection
- Establishing a safe space for sensitive topics
- Implementing teaching strategies that provide space for diverse viewpoints and encourage active, engaged listening.

Start with yourself

In order to create a classroom environment that can effectively support difficult conversations, we must start by striving to model constructive civil discourse ourselves. We have to be aware of our own strongly held biases, beliefs, political positions, and emotional responses, and be thoughtful about how they influence what we say and do when the headlines enter into the classroom.

As an educator who works with young people daily, you have both your own feelings to process, as well as concerns for your learners. Remember that you are not a neutral participant in your classroom, and you must take ownership of the lens that you bring to the classroom community. Learners may have experiences that are similar to or different from yours that inform their responses.

Educator and school leader Roy Hellenberg reflects on this important first step in addressing difficult topics in the classroom in an article he wrote to mark the tenth year of the Facing History and Ourselves and Shikaya partnership in South Africa in 2013:

> Growing up in South Africa, I was the youngest in my family. Despite that, when it came to arguing, no special consideration was afforded me. There were 13 of us, and family conversation often ranged from politics to religion, from education to human rights. Debates were won based on the strength of our arguments and the passion with which we communicated them.
>
> It was in these moments that I first learned one of the most important lessons of discussion: respect for the person you are

in conversation with. It was here that I learned to probe, prod, dissect, and dismantle the arguments of others. I realised the importance of respecting the views of others and the value in being open to re-evaluating my own preconceived ideas.

Today, as an educator, why do I value debate, differing viewpoints, and the rights of others to think differently than I do? In large part it is because of these early experiences — both with my family and in school. My high school History teacher held a viewpoint on the political situation in South Africa in the early 1980s that was different from the views held by my church leaders. My siblings embraced a host of beliefs and convictions that were different from my parents'. (I suspect this was because it was impossible for my parents to keep track of all 13 of us!) These dissenting voices helped me to develop the important skills of critical thinking and forced me to question myself and those around me. *Who do I believe? Why should I believe this point over that one? Why should I follow this ideology and not another?* It is this richness of opposing ideas that I wish to create in my classroom.

I try to foster this atmosphere in a number of ways. I approach teaching with an understanding that, as an educator, I am not a neutral conveyer of facts. I arrive at my classroom on any given day aware of my biases and value systems. Realising that I have my own predispositions and experiences allows me to "take them off", like a pair of spectacles. I can examine them and become aware of how they make me "see" the world. This makes me cautious and open to understanding that, even though I may have deeply held beliefs, they are simply choices I have made — they don't necessarily represent truth itself. My learners might hold a different truth from mine. The principal of my school might hold truths that are different from mine. The teacher in the classroom next door might hold different truths.

This understanding helps me create a classroom that is rich with opportunities for debate and encouraging of challenges. I am aware of some of the baggage I bring into the classroom; it's the baggage I'm not aware of that's problematic. I need to confront my own prejudices and values, because it's only when I confront my reality that I can allow learners to confront theirs.

I believe that young people are far more resilient than we often give them credit for. I show my learners that I will allow for my own views to be challenged, dissected, and even sometimes, discounted. This develops an environment of mutual respect where ideas, once voiced, become something we can all interact with, without it being attached to a particular ego or person.

Creating an environment that allows for democratic thinking and practices to emerge requires more than words. It requires that we, as teachers, live the values embodied in critical thinking. How can I expect learners to make themselves vulnerable and expose their ideas to criticism if I am not willing to do the same myself? How can I encourage my learners to become active citizens and challenge the people and practices that undermine democracy, and then fail to take any action myself in the face of injustice? Active citizenship that can transform communities and even countries requires first taking action in the immediate environment. Speaking up against "small" injustices often can be more impactful than looking for big causes to fight. Can we really tackle xenophobic violence when we turn a blind eye to bullying on the playground? Can we fight for a more accountable government if teachers at our own schools are not called to account? Teaching democratic values is not contained in a series of lessons; it is a lifestyle, an ethos that one creates in classrooms and the school as a whole.

To encourage active citizens who respect and value the democratic principles of our country's Constitution, it is important not only to pay attention to what happens in the classroom, but to also respect our learners' humanness in their lives beyond school and the four walls of the classroom. We must trust them to provide leadership. We must give them the time, space, and opportunity to grapple with these democratic values until they take root. We must spur them to action. And we must listen.

My job is to give my learners principles that will be of value to them throughout their lives. How do you live your life, in this world? How do you protect the basic principles of democracy, wherever you are? How do you ensure that you, as a democratic individual, live a life that's true to those beliefs and principles?

I don't know what my learners will encounter when they leave my classroom and my direct influence on their lives. But I know that there are many other South Africans who are eager to rise above their pasts, and that they are increasing in number. And as long as people like that exist in the world, I hope that my learners will encounter them and learn from their perspectives. I want them to be able to determine which views are worth having.

Develop a reflective classroom community

We cannot predict what will happen in our communities, our countries, or around the world that might elicit difficult questions from or spark heated debates between learners in our classrooms. But we can better prepare our learners to respond thoughtfully and respectfully together to such events by taking steps to cultivate a reflective classroom community throughout the school year.

A reflective classroom community is in many ways a microcosm of democracy – a place where explicit rules and implicit norms protect everyone's right to speak; where different perspectives can be heard and valued; where members take responsibility for themselves, each other, and the group as a whole; and where each member has a stake and a voice in collective decisions. Once established, both you and your learners will need to continue to nurture the reflective community on an ongoing basis through the ways that you participate and respond to each other.

We believe that a reflective, supportive classroom community is fostered by:

- creating a sense of trust and openness
- encouraging participants to speak and listen to each other
- making space and time for silent reflection
- offering multiple avenues for participation and learning
- helping learners appreciate the points of view, talents, and contributions of less vocal members.

Even the way we use the physical space in a classroom matters. Some arrangements promote a reflective community better than others. During a whole-class discussion, it is easier for learners to talk to each other when they can see each other's faces. Arranging the furniture in a circle promotes a sense of community and can make a difference. Likewise, placing chairs and desks in clusters for small-group work facilitates discussion. And then there's the wall space. Relevant pictures, posters, and learner work can play a role in generating a thoughtful atmosphere.

More than anything, mutual respect must be the cornerstone of the classroom environment. Can learners take risks? Will they be "shot down" or ridiculed by other learners, or even by the teacher, for openly sharing their thoughts? How will the teacher handle it when one learner personally insults or belittles another? Will they be respected and honoured as thoughtful participants in a community of learners? A teacher's behaviour in these situations sets the tone for the whole class. We need to be explicit and put into practice our belief that a deep respect for each learner is at the heart of our educational endeavour.

You can create the foundation for a safe community by jointly creating a classroom contract (see below). But you also need to make it clear that while you encourage the expression of different viewpoints and diverse voices, you will uphold a standard of civil discourse that keeps things safe for all participants. Given the tone of some public discourse in the press and social media, it is important to point out when things cross the line in order to create a safe community where you will expect and maintain a level of kindness and decency from all learners.

Create a classroom contract

One way to help classroom communities establish shared norms is by discussing them openly through a process called "contracting". Some teachers already customarily create classroom contracts with their learners at the start of each term. If you do not typically do so, we recommend that you engage your learners in creating one.

Contracts typically include several clearly defined rules or expectations for participation and consequences for those who do not fulfil their obligations as members of the learning community. Any contract created collaboratively by learners and the teacher should be consistent with the classroom rules already established by the teacher.

The following is a list of suggested items for your classroom contract. As you work together to create your own, you may want to discuss, include, or modify any or all of the items on this list:

- Listen with respect. Try to understand what someone is saying before rushing to judgement.
- Make comments using "I" statements. ("I disagree with what you said. Here's what I think.")
- If you do not feel safe making a comment or asking a question, write the thought down. You can ask the teacher after class to help you find a safe way to share the idea.
- If someone offers an idea or asks a question that helps your own learning, say "thank you".
- If someone says something that hurts or offends you, do not attack

the person. Acknowledge that the comment – not the person – hurt your feelings, and explain why.

- Put-downs are never okay.
- If you don't understand something, ask a question.
- Think with your head and your heart.
- Share talking time – provide room for others to speak.
- Do not interrupt others while they are speaking.
- Write down thoughts, in a journal or notebook, if you don't have time to say them during your time together.

We encourage you to frequently remind your learners that, regardless of the classroom strategy you are using or the topic you are addressing, it is essential that their participation honours the contract they helped create and follows your own classroom rules. In addition, we strongly recommend that you post the contract in a prominent location in your classroom and refer to its specific language when you redirect learners who stray from the guidelines set forth in the contract. You might find that when one learner deviates, others will respond by citing the specific expectations listed in the contract.

Provide opportunities for learner reflection

Before engaging in small- or whole-group discussion, provide learners with opportunities to formulate and process their ideas. Silence is one of the most powerful and underused tools in the classroom. Whether a teacher uses it to slow down his or her speech to emphasise a point, or adds an extended wait time after asking a question, silence can be invaluable. It creates space for thought and sends learners the message that we trust them as thoughtful individuals who need time to reflect.

As a tool for silent reflection, keeping a journal helps learners develop their ability to critically examine their surroundings from multiple perspectives and to make informed judgements about what they see and hear. Many learners find that writing or drawing in a journal helps them process ideas, formulate questions, and retain information. Journals make learning visible by providing a safe, accessible space for learners to share thoughts, feelings, and uncertainties. In this way, journals can also be an assessment tool – something teachers can review to better understand what their learners know, what they are struggling to understand, and how their thinking has changed over time.

In addition to strengthening learners' critical-thinking skills, journal writing serves other purposes. Journals help nurture classroom community. Through reading and commenting on journals, teachers build relationships with learners. Frequent journal writing also helps learners become more fluent in expressing their ideas in writing or speaking.

While there are many effective ways to use a journal as a learning tool, below are five questions that we suggest you consider:

1. *What is the teacher's relationship with learners' journals?* Will you read everything they write? Is it possible for them to keep something private? Will their journals be graded? If so, by what criteria? You can set limits on the degree to which you have access to learners' journals. Many teachers establish a rule that if learners wish to keep information in their journals private, they should fold the page over or remove the page entirely.

2. *What is appropriate content for journals?* It is easy for learners to confuse a class journal with a diary (or blog) because both formats allow for open-ended writing. Teachers should clarify how the audience and purpose for this writing are distinct from that of writing in a personal diary. To avoid uncomfortable situations, many teachers find it helpful to clarify topics that are not suitable material for journal entries. Also, teachers should explain that they are required to take certain steps, such as informing a school official, if learners reveal information about possible harm to themselves or another learner.

3. *How will journals be evaluated?* Many learners admit that they are less likely to share their true thoughts or express questions when they are worried about a grade based on getting the "right" answer or

using proper grammar or spelling. Therefore, we suggest that if you choose to grade learners' journals, which many teachers do, you base these grades on criteria such as effort, thoughtfulness, completion, creativity, curiosity, and making connections between the past and the present. Moreover, there are many ways to provide learners with feedback on their journals besides traditional grading, such as by writing comments or asking questions.

4. *What forms of expression can be included in a journal?* Learners learn and communicate best in different ways. The journal is an appropriate space to respect different learning styles. Some learners may wish to draw their ideas rather than record thoughts in words. Other learners may feel most comfortable responding in concept webs and lists instead of prose. When you introduce the journal to learners, you might brainstorm different ways that they might express their thoughts.

5. *How should journal content be publicly shared?* Most Facing History teachers have found that learners are best able to express themselves when they believe that their journal is a private space. Therefore, we suggest that information in learners' journals never be publicly shared without the consent of the writer. At the same time, we encourage you to provide multiple opportunities for learners to voluntarily share ideas and questions they have recorded. Some learners may feel more comfortable reading from their journals than speaking off the cuff in class discussions.

Establish a safe space for sensitive topics

Some topics can feel particularly difficult to address in the classroom – for example, issues related to race, immigration, and religion. Teachers can help learners practise having constructive, civil dialogue, characterised by listening respectively to multiple perspectives, but sometimes it is helpful to first acknowledge the possible discomfort of participants and reassure them that their feelings are valid and their contributions to the discussion are valuable.

The following activity is designed to help create a safe space. You can replace the word "race" with whatever sensitive topic you're focusing on.

1. Start with a journal prompt: Tell learners that the following writing exercise is a private journal entry that they will not be asked to share with anyone, so they should feel free to write their most honest reflection. Have learners take several minutes to complete this sentence: "I mostly feel _____ when discussing race, because _____."

2. Now that learners have gathered their thoughts, tell them that you are going to do a group brainstorm. They should not make "I" statements or share how they feel or what they wrote. Tell learners: "Let's put words on the board that represent the feelings that we think may be in the room when we discuss race. At this point, we will just list and not comment on them."

3. Now look at the list. Ask learners:
   - "What do the words have in common?" (Usually the words are mostly, but maybe not all, negative.)
   - "What else do you notice?" (The words are not just surface observations; they are deeply personal feelings.)
   - "Do you have any other important reflections?" (The words represent a wide and varied range of responses.)
   - "Which of these feelings are most valid?" (They are all valid. You may want to acknowledge that this is a rhetorical question, but it is important to validate everyone's feelings.)
   - "Where do these feelings come from?" (Personal experiences, the media, stereotypes, etc.)

4. It's important for teachers and learners to acknowledge that these feelings are in the room and that they need not be afraid of them. Each person should be allowed to enter this conversation wherever he or she is without being judged or shut down. Everyone needs to feel free to participate without fear of being called racist or given any other label.

Implement effective teaching strategies

The following teaching strategies can be particularly effective in facilitating discussions about controversial or sensitive topics. These strategies can create space for diverse viewpoints and encourage active listening and consideration of multiple perspectives.

1. Big Paper: Building a Silent Conversation
2. Save the Last Word for Me
3. Barometer: Taking a Stand on Controversial Issues
4. Four Corners Debate

Before using any of these strategies in the classroom, it is important to note that implementing specific teaching strategies alone will not produce thoughtful and productive class discussions. It is crucial that teachers carefully consider the questions, readings, or other materials they use to introduce and frame these activities and how those introductory materials connect to heated debates and partisan biases in current events.

Open-ended questions and resources that reflect the complexity and nuance often inherent in contemporary issues tend to lead to the most meaningful learning experiences for learners. Questions and resources that lead to specific conclusions or provoke learners' existing sensitivities or biases can be counterproductive. Teachers know their learners best and should carefully preview any materials that they will use for a class discussion to make sure that they lend themselves to meaningful, civil dialogue.

Big Paper: Building a Silent Conversation
Rationale

This discussion strategy uses writing and silence as tools to help learners explore a topic in depth. Having a written conversation with peers slows down the thinking process and gives learners an opportunity to focus on the views of others. This strategy also creates a visual record of thoughts and questions that can be referred to later. Using the Big Paper strategy can help engage shy learners who are not as likely to participate in a verbal discussion.

Procedure

1. Preparation
   a. Select the stimulus – the material that learners will respond to. As the stimulus for a Big Paper activity, teachers have used questions, quotations, historical documents, poetry, images, or excerpts from novels.
   b. Groups can be given the same stimulus for discussion; however, more often they are given different texts related to the same theme. This activity works best when learners are working in pairs or triads. Make sure that all learners have a pen or marker. Some teachers have learners use different colours to make it easier to see the back-and-forth flow of a conversation. Each group also needs a Big Paper (typically a sheet of poster paper) that can fit a written conversation and added comments. In the middle of the page, tape or write the stimulus (image, quotation, excerpt, etc.) that will be used to spark the learners' discussion.

2. The importance of silence
   a. Inform the class that this activity is completed in silence and all communication is done in writing. Tell learners that they will have time to speak in pairs and in large groups later. Before the activity begins, go over all of the instructions and ask learners if they have questions. This will avoid questions during the activity and minimise the chance that learners will interrupt the silence once it has begun. You can also remind learners of their task as they begin each new step.

3. Comment on your Big Paper
   a. Each group receives a Big Paper; each learner receives a marker or pen. The groups read the text in silence. After learners have

finished, they may comment on the text and ask questions of each other in writing on the Big Paper. The written conversation must start on the text but can stray to wherever the learners take it. If someone in the group writes a question, another member should address it by writing on the Big Paper. Learners can draw lines connecting a comment to a particular question. Make sure learners know that more than one of them can write on the Big Paper at the same time. The teacher can determine the length of this step, but it should be at least 15 minutes.

4. Comment on other Big Papers

    a. Still working in silence, learners leave their partner(s) and walk around reading the other Big Papers. Learners bring their marker or pen and can write comments or further questions for thought on other Big Papers. Again, the teacher can determine the length of time for this step based on the number of Big Papers and his or her knowledge of the learners.

5. Return to your own Big Paper

    a. The silence is broken. The learners rejoin back at their own Big Paper. They should look at any comments written by others. Now they can have a free, verbal conversation about the text, their own comments, what they read on other papers, and comments that their fellow learners wrote back to them. You might ask learners to take out their journals and identify a question or comment that stands out to them at this moment.

6. Class discussion

    a. Finally, debrief the process with the large group. The conversation can begin with a simple prompt such as, "What did you learn from doing this activity?" This is the time to delve deeper into the content and use ideas from the Big Papers to bring out learners' thoughts. The discussion can also touch upon the importance and difficulty of staying silent and the level of comfort with this activity.

Save the Last Word for Me

Rationale

This discussion strategy requires all learners to participate as active speakers and listeners. Its clearly defined structure helps shy learners share their ideas and ensures that frequent speakers practise being quiet. It is often used as a way to help learners debrief a reading or film.

Procedure

1. Preparation
    a. Identify a reading or video excerpt that will serve as the catalyst for this activity.

2. Learners read and respond
    a. Have learners read or view the selected text. Ask learners to highlight three sentences that particularly stand out for them and to write each sentence on the front of an index card. On the back, they should write a few sentences explaining why they have chosen that quote – what it means to them, reminds them of, etc. They may connect it to something that has happened to them in their own life, to a film or book they saw or read, or to something that has happened in history or is happening in current events.

3. Sharing in small groups
    a. Divide learners into groups of three, labelling one learner A, one B, and the other C. Invite Learner A to read one of her chosen quotations and talk about why she chose it. Give the learner a set amount of time, perhaps a minute, to speak. During that minute, Learners B and C listen; they do not interrupt or interject. After the minute, Learner B gets a chance to speak for one minute. He can both expand on Learner A's thinking, say what questions it raised for him, provide a different idea, or challenge the thinking of Learner A. When Learner B talks, Learners A and C listen; they do not interrupt or clarify. After Learner B has a minute, Learner C gets a turn to speak without interruption. Finally, Learner A

gets one minute to answer questions or respond to the other learners' ideas. In this way, Learner A gets the last word.

b. The intent of this exercise is to create equity in a discussion and for learners to practise moments of listening without trying to immediately respond.

c. Each learner should get a chance to start a round of conversation with the quote or phrase they pulled from the text and have the last word. After each learner has had a turn, you may want to open up the class to a larger, freeform discussion in order to process all the structured discussions that the smaller groups had.

Barometer: Taking a Stand on Controversial Issues

Rationale

This teaching strategy helps learners share their opinions by lining up along a continuum to represent their point of view. It is especially useful when trying to discuss an issue about which learners have a wide range and variety of opinions.

Procedure

1. Preparation

    a. Identify a space in the classroom where learners can create a line or a U-shape. Place "Strongly Agree" and "Strongly Disagree" signs at opposite ends of a continuum in your room. Or you can post a statement and then, at the other end of the line, post its opposite.

2. Contracting

    a. Set a contract for this activity. Since it deals with learners literally putting themselves and their opinions on the line, it has the potential for outbursts that result from some not understanding how classmates can hold certain opinions. Reiterate your class rules about respect for the opinions and voices of others and call for them to be honest, but not insulting. Readdress ways to constructively disagree with one another, and require that when offering their opinion or defence of their stance, they speak from the "I" rather than from an accusatory "You".

3. Formulating an opinion

   a. Give learners a few minutes to reflect on a prompt that calls for agreement or disagreement with a particular statement. Facing History teachers often have learners respond to the prompt in their journals.

4. Take a stand

   a. Ask learners to stand on the spot of the line that represents their opinion, telling them that if they stand on either extreme, they are absolute in their agreement or disagreement. They may also stand anywhere in between the two extremes, depending on how much they do or do not agree with the statement.

5. Explain positions

   a. Once learners have lined up, ask them to explain why they have chosen to stand where they are. Encourage learners to refer to evidence and examples when defending their stance. It is probably best to alternate from one end to the middle to the other end, rather than allowing too many voices from one stance to dominate. After about three or four viewpoints are heard, ask if anyone wishes to move. Encourage learners to keep an open mind; they are allowed to move if someone presents an argument that alters where they want to stand on the line. Run the activity until you feel that most or all voices have been heard, making sure that one person does not dominate.

6. Debriefing

   a. There are many ways to debrief this exercise. You can have learners reflect in their journals about how the activity changed or reinforced their original opinion. Or you can chart the main for and against arguments on the board as a whole-class activity.

Four Corners Debate

Rationale

Four Corners Debate is a variation on the Barometer teaching strategy (see page 197). Similarly, it requires learners to show their position on a specific statement (Strongly Agree, Agree, Disagree, Strongly Disagree) by standing in a particular corner of the room. This activity elicits the participation of all learners by requiring everyone to take a position. Drawing out learners' opinions on a topic they are about to study can be a useful warm-up activity. Asking them to apply what they have learned when framing arguments can be an effective follow-through activity.

Procedure

1. Preparation
    a. Label the four corners of the room with signs reading: "Strongly Agree", "Agree", "Disagree", "Strongly Disagree". Generate a list of controversial statements related to the material being studied. Statements most likely to encourage discussion typically do not have one correct or obvious answer, elicit nuanced arguments (e.g. "This might be a good idea some of the time, but not all of the time"), and represent respected values on both sides of the debate.
2. Introduce statements
    a. Distribute statements and give learners the opportunity to respond to them in writing. Many teachers provide a graphic organiser or worksheet that requires learners to mark their opinion (Strongly Agree, Agree, Disagree, Strongly Disagree) and then provide a brief explanation.
3. Four Corners discussion
    a. After learners have considered their personal response to the statements, read one of the statements aloud, and ask learners to move to the corner of the room that best represents their opinion. Once learners are in their places, ask for volunteers to justify their position. When doing so, they should refer to evidence

from history or sources they've been studying as well as other relevant information from their own experiences. Encourage learners to switch corners if someone presents an idea that causes a change of mind. After a representative from each corner has defended his or her position, you can allow learners to question each other's evidence and ideas. Before beginning the discussion, remind learners about norms for having a respectful, open discussion of ideas.

4. Reflection

   a. There are many ways to debrief this exercise. You can have learners reflect in their journals about how the activity changed or reinforced their original opinion. Some of their views may have been strengthened by the addition of new evidence and arguments, while others may have changed altogether. It is quite possible that some learners will be more confused or uncertain about their views after the Four Corners Debate. While uncertainty can feel uncomfortable, it is an important part of the understanding process and represents an authentic wrestling with moral questions that have no clear right or wrong answers. To clarify ideas shared during the discussion, you can chart the main for and against arguments on the board as a whole-class activity.

Additional resources to foster civil discourse

Here are some additional resources to help you foster open, thoughtful, and respectful dialogue in your classroom. Please visit the website, facinghistory.org, to learn more about the full range of services that Facing History offer for professional development and resources to support every stage of your career as an educator.

• Subscribe to the blog, Facing Today (facingtoday.facinghistory.org) to hear each week from teachers, learners, staff, and supporters with practical tips about using Facing History in the classroom and the world. Some related posts you may want to review include:

- "How Teachers Can Help Students Make Sense of Today's Political and Social Tensions"
- "8 Components of a Reflective Classroom"
- "Hope Will Never Be Silent"
- "Creating Space for Student Voices"
- "Teaching in a Time of Terrorism"
- "After Eric Garner: One School's Courageous Conversation".

- Explore Facing History's collection of 60 learner-centred teaching strategies that engage young people of all learning styles. Help learners become responsible consumers and producers of news and information by understanding the role of confirmation bias in how they interpret news and information, weighing the impact of social media on the traditional news cycle, learning how to verify sources of information, and considering their responsibilities as citizens in a democracy. Explore the post "Facing Ferguson: News Literacy in a Digital Age".

- Bolster conversations about difficult societal issues by approaching them through the lens of history and literature. Not only can this help learners better understand the roots and underlying nuances of these issues, but such an approach can also provide some distance to explore issues of human behaviour in the past while allowing time for learners to make connections to our world today. Facing History's core case studies integrate history and human behaviour in order to help learners think critically about the choices they make every day and about how they want to participate in the world. Examples that relate to the South African school curriculum include:
  - "Choices in Little Rock" (The US Civil Rights Movement)
  - "Race and Membership" (The Eugenics Movement)
  - "Holocaust and Human Behavior" (Nazi Germany and the Holocaust)
  - "Teaching Mockingbird" (*To Kill a Mockingbird*).

These can be accessed at www.facinghistory.org. Visit www.shikaya.org for more information about Facing History's work in South Africa.

ACKNOWLEDGEMENTS

We are indebted to everyone we interviewed on camera for this book. We thank you for your courage to be open, to be vulnerable and honest, and to share your experience so generously.

This book would not have been possible without the generous and ongoing support of The Federated Employer's Mutual Assurance Company who continue to put improving South African schools at the forefront of their efforts. In particular we would like to thank Ashwin Daya for his early belief in this project and his efforts to make this happen.

Thank you to Alycia Habana, Daniel Hellenberg, Luvuyo Maseko and Peter Manser who early on gave of their time and experiences in our research phase. Thanks to Samantha Kriger and Cyrill Walters who took the time to read the early drafts and offer their honest and valuable insight. Thank you to Lynda Jones for prioritising our transcriptions and to Leah Nasson who helped us make sense of the interviews.

Books are more than the words that end up on the pages before us. There is a team that put this book together. Thank you to Louise Grantham, Russell Clarke and Nicola van Rooyen at Bookstorm for getting the idea into the pages and onto the shelves. Thank you, Wesley Thompson, for looking at this with the fresh eyes of an editor and gently pruning our thoughts and words.

Thank you to Luke Younge, who delivered the interviews onto film. Not only is he masterful behind a lens and an editing suite, but the humility and authenticity he also brings to his work allows for the people he films to shine.

We are indebted to the support and generosity of Facing History and Ourselves who allowed us to include one of their resources in this book and who continue to work with us in creating schools where all feel they belong.

Karen Murphy, Gail Weldon and Marc Skvirsky have been with us in our work in schools right from the start. Their vision began this journey and their support, guidance and friendship over the last fifteen years has helped us put our pens to paper.

Finally, if books are more than the words you see on this paper, these authors are so much more than three South African men. We each have a brood of children who give us hope that the future South Africa can be better than our past. And we each have someone who ends up carrying the load when we are typing away, who offers us the honest feedback that we need and who reminds us that life exists when we eventually look up.

REFERENCES

Berry, J (2004), "What Do We Do with a Variation?," in *Only One of Me: Selected Poems*, London: Macmillan Children's Books.

Binkovitz, L (24 April 2017), "Why Black and Brown Students need Black and Brown Teachers", *Houston Chronicle*. Available at https://www.houstonchronicle.com/local/gray-matters/article/Why-black-and-brown-students-need-black-and-brown-11089875.php.

BusinessTech (13 July 2016), "Shocking Pay Difference Between Black and White Professionals in South Africa". Available at https://businesstech.co.za/news/business/129980/shocking-difference-in-pay-between-black-and-white-professionals-in-sa/.

Facing History and Ourselves, "Creating 'We and They': Kwame Anthony Appiah", interview with Facing History and Ourselves (Undated). Available at: https://www.facinghistory.org/resource-library/video/creating-we-and-they-kwame-anthony-appiah.

Facing History and Ourselves, "John Amaechi Discusses Identity", interview with Facing History and Ourselves (2014). Available at: https://www.facinghistory.org/resource-library/video/john-amaechi-discusses-identity.

Facing History and Ourselves, *Fostering Civil Discourse – A Guide for Classroom Conversations*. Available at www.facinghistory.org.

Greyling, J (17 May 2017), "Constitution Says Religion can be Practiced 'at', Not 'by' Schools, Court Hears''. Available at https://www.news24.com/SouthAfrica/News/constitution-says-religion-can-be-practiced-at-not-by-schools-court-hears-20170517.

Kandola, B (2009), *The Value of Difference: Eliminating Bias in the Workplace*, Kidlington: Pearn Kandola Publishing.

Ladson-Billings, G (19 January 2015), "Ladson-Billings examines, 'What if we had more black teachers?'", University of Wisconsin-Madison. Available at https://www.education.wisc.edu/soe/news-events/news/2015/01/19/ladson-billings-examines---what-if-we-had-more-black-teachers-.

Netflix, "Expensing, Entertainment, Gifts and Travel Policy". Available at https://jobs.netflix.com/culture/#introduction.

Project Implicit (2011), "Project Implicit FAQs". Available at https://implicit.harvard.edu/implicit/demo/background/faqs.html#faq7.

NOTES

NOTES

NOTES